It makes a lot of sense to start off with called "Private Equity Investing - Leveraged Buyouts" or something like that off the Barnes and Noble shelf. A Boeing sized tome that weighed more than the chair I sat on. The text size was small, the examples were ridiculously complex, and the ideas sounded utterly alien to everyone but the deeply experienced.

Okay, so maybe starting out with that one was a little too ambitious. I picked up a pamphlet on leveraged buyout modeling, thinking that it would help me understand how they did their deals and made their money. It came with a huge Excel file that I thought I could pick through. But a massive model like that makes no sense if nobody sits by you, holds your hand and walks you through that mess of numbers. That was not helpful either. I realized that I was going to have to pick it up on the fly.

So I went about it.

It was a real pain. Every day during work, I noted puzzling term after puzzling term in a small gray notebook. Every day after work I sat at my computer and Googled every term. Wrote down every definition in neat, little script. "Neat" because I had to come back to it again. "Little" because there was **a lot** of terms. Limited partner. Institutional investor. Prime brokerage. Total Return Swap. PIPE. Incentive Fee. Management Fee. RMB Denominated Fund. Junk Bond. Request for Information. Spinoff. Event Driven. Risk Arb (arbitrage). Repurchase Agreements. Futures. Global Macro.

Two steps forward, one step back. You have to immerse yourself in it and soak like beef in marinade. Right up to the point where you make jokes in the lingo. To the point where you find it crossing over into your conversations with your non-work friends. To the point where it stops feeling like a third arm coming out of your neck.

Then one day I sat with a person in the industry and she decided to challenge me with a question straight out of an interview.

"What is venture capital?"

Three answers came to mind. I took the time to count them myself. Well it could be that but then it could also be that unless when this is in effect. They rose up so fast they jammed themselves up in my head and I had no idea which one to start off with. Should I give just the most commonly known one or list all three with their individual contingent conditions?

The second those three bubbled up, I knew. That was it. That was the moment I was starting to get it together.

And it had taken way too long to get there.

Here are the places I had to work at before that day. A business brokerage catering to private equity funds. A valuation firm marking private companies. A small private equity firm. An investment advisory firm. A large hedge fund's investor relations department. An accounting firm specialized in auditing only hedge funds.

In the end, I figured there had to be something easier out there.

This work started out as a Google Doc with stuff I jotted down late at night before I went to bed. Just a letter to a friend with a passing interest in the topic. She eventually got her letter but the thing kept growing like a weed and soon I decided that I wanted to make it into something more formal. A book, perhaps.

But I did not want to go through all that trouble and spend all that time if it did not serve a purpose. Before I started on anything I sat down and found five reasons that a novice should read my work over something else. I taped the list above my iMac and so helpful they were in keeping me on track through the long and difficult birthing process that I thought that I would post them here for you to take in:

1) When I started back in the dark days, I found big long books with too much information to be helpful. I also found investing memoirs by hedge fund managers which featured great stories but were looking to entertain rather than to help me learn. I also found "trade like the pros" manuals that tried to sell me on an investing style. Those were not helpful for anyone in any way. This is a short easy read that gets you from point A to B immediately.

2) The thoughts, observations, and discussions in this book come right out of the workplace. I pulled subjects from lunchtime conversations, midday rants, and late night talk in the office. It is not stuffy academic material written by a professor in the ivory tower. It is not a bland accounting analysis by a billionaire hedge fund manager. I wanted to make this writing earthy and topical. This is the kind of stuff that people in the industry think about, stress out on, and ponder over everyday.

4

3) The "Starting Off" section, which comprises of this book's first four chapters, is the only thing you should read first. After that, anything you do not care for you can skip. You can read the private equity section first if you wish. Or the hedge fund section if that is your cat's fancy. Everything is cut into smaller sections with informative titles and "let's get to the point" writing. It is for you. Drop and pick up whenever it is convenient for you.

4) This book is not going to cost you an arm and a leg. You put down a good $80 for a textbook and even $16 for a journalistic expose on the hedge fund industry. The up front cost for this one is nowhere near that amount.

5) A personal message at the very end, with the best career advice I ever gave to anyone and a simple moral lesson that I wish I knew from the first day of my career. Especially important for those who want to actually make a living in the industry. Most people I meet seem to want to. I hope one inspires you and the other actually helps you.

Five reasons I gave myself to write this book. I hope these same five can move you to read it.

The book starts off with the recommended preamble on hedge funds and private equity. There we talk about portfolio theory, limited partners, and fees. Then I talk about some select hedge fund strategies like high frequency trading and event-driven. Following that is a bit on bonds and derivatives. I walk you through it to make it as easy to understand and I think it is important for a full understanding of the markets. Next comes private equity featuring a comprehensive example of a leveraged buyout. At the end is my conclusion; a short moral message and some work commandments.

Feel free to skip around to whatever is your fancy. Not like these words are going to disappear from the page anytime soon.

As you read, if you come across anything that may seem puzzling to you or for some reason does not jive with what you already know or have read in the news, step back for a second and think about why that might be the case. Perhaps special circumstances dictated an exception. If that is the case then you can make an excellent educational opportunity out of comparing what you know and what is in here. Or perhaps I am just wrong. If that is the case then and you feel like helping a friend out, feel free to reach out to me via email and let me know. I would love to hear from you.

Now enough chatter from me. Let's go!

What are Hedge Funds and Private Equity Funds?

The Basics

This probably is the toughest part of the book because it is the point where you make that first leap into the alternative asset management world. It is kind of like making a cannonball dive into a freezing cold lake - some things are definitely going to make your teeth chatter. And since I start building on these terms real fast in the next few chapters I thought I should pause you here for a second and tell you what you can expect in this chapter. **My learning philosophy is that the more times you see a phrase and its definitions repeated, the faster you start to get it.** For most documents I know, that means reading some long droning passage over and over again. I hate that, so I am going to do my best to have you avoid that.

You can expect this chapter to go in this sort of direction:

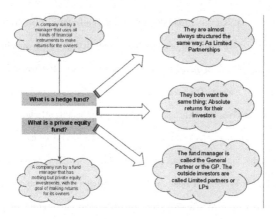

The above graphic tells you everything you know about this whole chapter. This is what you need to know and keep in mind because we build on this. If all of it is already familiar to you then feel free to skip ahead to the next chapter, which discusses the fees that hedge and private equity funds charge their clients. That chapter immediately starts using some of the terminology I introduce here. However, any of this looks alien to you then keep on reading and know that **you already are starting to get it**.

***

What are hedge funds? **They are largely unregulated business partnerships investing money in hope of obtaining absolute returns.** They are companies like just like any other you might imagine, founded and operated by a fund manager (sometimes also called a portfolio manager), but their entire business is to take in money from outside investors for investing.

I understand that that is a very broad definition. **Such a broad definition and a general lack of understanding as to what these things really are has led to the term being thrown around willy nilly.** In my opinion the original definition has been long made useless. The first hedge funds were called as such because they differentiated themselves from mutual funds by having the power to hedge some of their investments by shorting stocks.[1] Today, there are mutual funds that can short stocks too and there are hedge funds that do not short at all. Therefore the definition has been diluted to such that the term "hedge fund" is just kind of a catch-all phrase for investment companies seeking absolute returns. What "absolute return" means I will get to in a second.

Next, a private equity fund. This is easier to understand. Private equity refers to a type of transaction, a classification. **A private equity fund is just a fund (again, a business set up by a manager to take in money) entirely made up of private equity investments.** So what makes a transaction a private equity transaction? It is a diagnosis of exclusion. **A private equity transaction can be called as such if it involves the purchase or sale of securities that are not publicly traded on the market.**

***

---

[1] To remind you, they are people skeptic about the stock's ability to continue collecting price gains in the future. They borrow the stock through their brokers and sell it. They keep the money but know that eventually they have to return the borrowed item, the stock, to close the trade. If the price goes down then they get to keep the difference between the cost of repurchasing the stock back to close the trade and the money they got from the first sale.

Achieving absolute returns is a very specific thing. Every year the market (usually defined as the S&P500 or the Russell 3000, just every possible investable stock out there) goes up or goes down, returning a number. Some years it is positive. Some years it is negative.

These market returns matter for people seeking "relative returns", where you just want to beat the market. **Mutual funds seek to achieve relative returns.** They are a much larger industry with more regulation. Their threshold is the market, so it is okay with them if they end the year with a negative return if the market did a bigger negative that year.

Hedge and private equity funds do not care about the market and are not judged by the market. Their clients have very high expectations; they want their investments to grow in value every year without fail. A mutual fund with a negative return can point to the market and tell their investors that it was a bad year for everyone. They can do that and their investors can understand because for a mutual fund seeking relative returns, how the market does matters.

Hedge funds do not really have that excuse. If the market is negative, their clients want to be positive. If the market is positive, their clients want an even higher positive. It seems like an ambitious goal and certainly nobody should ever think that it is an easy job to hit those goals year in and year out.[2] Yet managers have done it before and are

---

[2] There is a phrase I hear that describes this and it is called "Alpha". Alpha is defined as the return someone can get you above and beyond the normal market return. You can calculate it too and make a number out of it, which excites the statheads. Perhaps it is just my own personal experience but I have never heard this phrase used by the hedge fund professionals that I have worked with unless it is in a marketing context.

motivated to do so with very fat fees. In addition, funds are authorized to use every sort of financial instrument available to do their business. What some of those instruments might be I will expand upon in the coming chapters.

***

I find it very helpful to imagine these funds not as "funds" but as "companies". Like any other type of business they have income statements and balance sheets. They take money from their investors to buy things which they hope can make them profits. The amount of profit that the company makes at the end of the year gets charged certain fees (the details of which are in the next chapter) and is then reported to the investors as the fund's year end return. These profits can either be funneled back into the company or returned to the investors. Funds, hedge and private equity alike, are companies and if you keep this metaphor in mind then it makes the next concept I look to explain, that involving limited partnerships, much easier to take in.

Companies can choose to be structured in many different ways. Such structures affect how the company's owners are taxed by the government and can also protect those owners from becoming liable for the misdeeds and damages that the business might have caused (the latter concept's idea of limiting what is liable is why it is often called "limited liability"). In fact, the way we classify every type of business structure by their differences regarding the tax and limited liability implications. **Hedge funds and private equity funds frequently set themselves up in a specific way: As a limited partnership.** Let me break that down for you.

A partnership is defined as a business with many owners, the partners. A limited partnership is a special type of partnership, a sub-classification. The very distinct thing about it is its two types of partners: Limited and general partners.

There must always be a general partner. He runs the partnership and without him there is no partnership. **The fund dissolves if the general partner for some reason disappears.** This entity runs the company and because of that shoulders *"unlimited liability"*. The limited partners do not get involved in the operation of the business - they only bring in the money and get out of the way. Their limited participation in the operation of the business means that limited partners cannot lose any more than what they brought in. The business term for that is "limited liability". If partnership for some reason (like some sort of court decision that goes against their way) owes an amount that is greater than the Limited Partners' investment, then the difference is made up by the general partner.

In applying these concepts to a hedge or private equity fund, the general partner is the fund manager and the limited partners are the outside investors. People in the industry commonly use the phrases GP and LP for short. I will do the same.

So right now where are we? In this section we found that hedge funds and private equity funds are nothing more than companies seeking to achieve absolute returns for their LPs. They take on a special business structure authorized by the government, the limited partnership. The limited partnership is defined by two types of owners. These two types are called the general partner and the limited partner. The general partner is the fund manager and is the fearless leader guiding the fund forward. The limited partners bring in the money and watch with a paternal eye.

Like I said, this is the first step. If you still feel wobbly about anything, go back to the graphic and look at it again. Or go do something else and come back. Let it stew in your head for a while. I did not write this book to make it a chore, so do not let it be one for you.

Up next: I am going to talk about how the fund managers (or the general partners or the GPs) of the funds get paid.

How Do People In Asset Management Get Paid?

Hint: They are not paid goats from Kazakhstan.

Here I am going to talk about fees, the charges the GP collect. These are the payments made by the LPs (the outside investors) to the fund manager so that the investor can see his total investment grow. So why did I make this the topic that comes right after the introduction? I want to have you get immediately familiar with some more language. Fee language and concepts are universal to all funds. You can drop the term "incentive fee" in a finance-oriented conversation without sounding like an idiot.

One other reason I wanted to put this here is because most everyone knows about the godly rich hedge fund manager. They have become a common character in Hollywood movies and romance novels. People have started to associate the role with just plain "riches". How such riches are obtained is glossed over. Here, you are going to learn where all that money comes from. Wealthy hedge fund or private equity fund managers, their fortunes start to made through these fees from big outside investors. Later on though, I am going to tell you that the dynamic reverses. Soon the fund managers become their own biggest investors, making themselves wealthy by investing their own huge sums.

Some of the other things you can expect to figure out here are:

~ **What are incentive and management fees and what are they paying for?**

~ **What is with those billion dollar paydays anyway?**

~ **When is a 100% return not enough to earn an incentive fee?**

~ **How can a big fund screw its investors over with its management fees?**

~ **Why do investors stick with big funds then?**

Much more as well but that is soon to come. Right now, let us walk through the kind of money you as a fund investor can expect to pay the person running your fortunes.

***

Funds are paid through two types of fees, <u>a management fee</u> and <u>an incentive fee</u>. The management fee is the money paid by the limited partners (the investors) to the general partner (the fund manager) for the trouble of managing their money. It is calculated by taking a certain percentage of the total assets at the beginning of the year, the most common number seems to be 2%.

Incentive fees are taken out of a fund's profit for the year. Profit? Remember that a hedge fund, private equity fund, or venture capital fund is a business. They have money brought in by their partners and they invest it so to make more money. **The extra money that is brought in by their investing activities is profit and becomes subject to the incentive fee.** This fee tends to be pegged at 20% but varies depending on the quality of the GP. Top hedge funds with high performance ability get to charge more because of their proven record, sometimes up to 40%.

What does all this money pay for? Asset management firms are not expensive to set up in a practical sense. You rent an office, pay a prime brokerage a certain amount, and you are pretty much ready to go. No factories or heavy equipment to bring in. Probably the most expensive piece of equipment is the Bloomberg terminal, a desktop computer that brings financial types a wealth of up-to-date facts and figures. People swear by it and thanks to their cost (thousands of dollars a month!) they make great status symbols. **These hang-the-slate expenses as well as the year end bonus pool for the regular employees (operations managers who make trades happen smoothly, accountants, and more) are paid from the management fee.**

Incentive fees go to the owners of the asset management firm. This is in part because incentive fees are very volatile from year to year and regular employees would be very unappreciative if they found their bonus pool vaporizing with a down market. It also aligns the incentives of the managers with the LPs. The partners of the fund management company get paid the most when their fund is successful. This means that no one gets cheated out if the fund returns suck.

***

One of the tougher concepts I tried to tackle regarding hedge fund operations is the "high water mark". It is a policy that is used by a fund's investor to keep from being fraudulently charged fees for performance that looks better than it really is. To explain it to you, I would like to go through an extended setup.

Do you have a brokerage account and do a little investing of your own on the side? If so, then you probably keep track of your annual percentage returns. If your friend tells you he made a 50% gain last year, then you probably would be very impressed and you would think that he has made himself quite wealthy. **However, if he then accidentally drops the fact that he lost 90% the year before that, then your estimation of his wealth slips dramatically.** He is not in fact any richer. He might even be poorer than he was two years ago. The point is that the context matters. A high return number does not mean anything to what really is important - the actual amount of money in the bank - if it is prefaced by a huge loss the previous year.

Let us move from people to funds. Imagine that Big Roller Fund has some LPs and one LP's share of the portfolio is worth $1M in the open market. That's great! But in 2008, the financial crisis ate away 50% of the account's value. Now the LP has $500K worth of investments. That's sad but next year the managers grit their teeth and ride a great market all the way back to $1M. They returned 100% in 2009! That's great! Now time to sit back and start working on figuring out those incentive fees, right?

Wrong. The same thing you realized with your friend applies here with Big Roller Fund. **No way should any manager be paid an incentive fee for merely doing nothing more than returning an LP's investment back to where it was before.** Nobody would invest in a fund that would try to shanghai you into that sort of deal. So GPs introduced the concept of the high water mark: Big Roller Fund's manager does not get paid unless his LP gets a return on his investment. I have a simple graphic here to illustrate the concept for you:

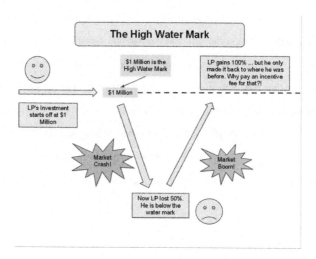

Now that you are done laughing at how bad this graphic is, let us talk our way through it.

Big Roller Fund's high water mark starts off at $1M - the highest number it ever reached in the life of the account. The incentive fees get charged only if the account grows beyond that number. Growing $500K to $1M after losing $500K last year? No fee. $1M to $2M? Because now the LP has seen his investment make progress, the GP can justify charging an incentive fee. We can calculate it by taking the $2M ending amount and subtracting the $1M high water mark, and then taking 20% to end up with a smooth $200K.

Add to that the 2% management fee, the amount of which is calculated from total fund assets at the beginning of the year, and you find that the GP has made for itself in fees $220,000. **Considering that the fund started the year with $1,000,000, the fund manager basically charged his investors a fifth of the entire fund in a single year.** Now, this is only the case because Big Roller made a 100% return and a fund does not often make those but it gives a sense of how big of a carrot the incentive fee can be. A big incentive fee means that the GP and the LPs are on the same page. Knowing this, the LPs, though irked by the high cost, ante up. You get what you pay for.

***

Imagine what it must be like to earn a <u>billion dollars in pay in just a single year</u>. For comparison consider JK Rowling, the author of the Harry Potter novels, who ignited a worldwide craze lasting over a decade and "only" earned $700 million. John Paulson is estimated to have personally made $3.7 billion in 2007 *alone*, when his funds made ridiculous returns shorting the subprime mortgage market. His funds returned over 100%. Three years later in 2010, Paulson earned $5 billion dollars. His returns, though still impressive, were not as high as they were in 2007 - the information is private but news reports say around 45%. 2010's return is much lower than 2007's 100% plus. **What gives? He arguably did a better job in 2007 but got a billion dollars less.**

First, let me say that these calculations are just that: Calculations and speculations. We do not know the real number because the company is privately held. Beyond that, though, the number is disingenuous. **It implies that someone got paid $5 billion in a year by his company like as if John opened his mailbox one day and a $5 billion check fell out fluttering to his feet.** Not exactly. People calculated this differently from a mere paycheck. The $5 billion payday includes the returns made on money Paulson had in his own fund.

A hedge fund often starts out with a little bit of the GP's money in it. The majority of the fund is made up of the LP's money. As time passes, the GP accumulates wealth via incentive and management fees. The LPs withdraw to pay their obligations. The fund closes itself off to new investors. **What happens is that after many years of successful returns, the GP ends up his own biggest client, essentially becoming a massive brokerage account for the GP and their employees.**

This is why the news reports can say Paulson made $5 billion in 2010. The news reports counted the money he made off investing his own huge holdings as part of his "paycheck". It is kind of like saying that you made $10,000 returning 20% on your $50,000 brokerage account. Yes, one can still say it is "income," (the IRS will certainly argue so) but it is not a paycheck nor is it a wad of cash from one party to another. Regardless, it is still a whole lot of money no matter what form it comes in.

I have this here to clear up a common misconception and one I myself held early in my studies. It is an easy error to make but one just as easy to fix. And you just did it!

(A bit of John Paulson follow up through 2013. While Paulson did incredibly well with his single bet on subprime bonds and his second move on shorting banks during the financial crisis of 2008, his picks since then have, to say the least, disappointed. Paulson's funds bet big on an economic recovery in 2011, but the big recovery did not come and his bets on banks - especially Bank of America - have not panned out. Another one of this stock picks, Sino-Forest, was accused of accounting fraud and lost nearly all of its value in a single day! In the end, his Advantage Plus fund lost 51% in 2011. Then in 2012, he invested against the European sovereign-debt crisis, betting that it would get worse. Instead, things in Europe calmed down and through the first 10 months of 2012 Advantage Plus lost another 17%.)

Still, fees and especially management fees at big funds are becoming a point of contention between GPs and prospective LPs. Remember, management fees are paid even if the fund does not do well during the year. They are charged no matter what and they do add up: Some of the largest hedge funds in the United States have over <u>$20 billion</u> under management. 2% of $20 billion is a cool <u>$400 million</u> right off the bat.

The sheer size of the management fee raises questions that you as a potential LP cannot ignore. Are you investing on the basis of the fund's management, performance, or on how impressive the fund firm's manager-CEO-founder can be in a presentation? If so, are you going to like what your management fees are paying for?

Here is a common situation. A retired titan of industry has several million dollars that he wants to turbocharge with a hedge fund. Mr. Titan likes to read the paper and has read several good articles about a smart man running Awesome Fund. He decides that he will make an investment. Who is he really investing with, the fund or the man? Mr. Titan thinks he is investing with the man.

More often than not, Awesome Fund is a very large fund with many billions of dollars under management. Perhaps at one time its manager, Mr. Awesome, ran that fund day to day, doing his own research and picking the stocks himself. Now that Awesome Fund is billions of dollars large, it is likely that Mr. Awesome is no longer doing as hands on as he used to be at the fund's inception. The life of a hedge fund manager is stressful and Mr. Awesome is getting older - perhaps he wants to look after his kids or play with his boat out in the Caribbean. He starts passing off day to day duties to others in the firm but stays as the fund's main figurehead and publicity figure. He comes in to shake hands with a potential LP to lock in their commitment and makes appearances on TV for smart economy-related blurbs. **The actual money running and portfolio managing is left to his proteges.** Mr. Titan thinks that the Mr. Awesome who shook his hand and gave him a great presentation is the one calling the shots, but more often than not he is wrong.

Is Mr. Titan being gypped? Should he really be expecting that Mr. Awesome should call every order himself? You could say so. He invests in Awesome Fund based on its manager's talent and talent in the hedge fund community is everything. A good portfolio manager is a truly special thing and much harder to find than you would think. **If Mr. Awesome checks out of day to day managing who is going to carry the burden of delivering that annual 25%?** Are his proteges good enough? Making big returns with huge amounts of money really is a different game. Warren Buffett complains about it every year; it is a lot harder to manage billions than millions. The investable market is much smaller. People watch your every move, copying your investments. You need to find huge successes to move the needle. And if you actually pull it off, you end up having to do it again next year and this time with even more money.

If the team does a wonderful job and the fund beats the market - meets those absolute returns - then that is great. Then nobody cares about the management fees, really. **What usually happens though is that Mr. Awesome continues to fund-raise like a mad man but the LPs find themselves with mediocre returns year in and year out.** Mr. Awesome is satisfied enough with just raking in the management fees and does not take the arduous extra steps to get the maximum possible return for their LPs.

Not like LPs are just going to sit around and let that happen to them. My father once argued with a hotel clerk over a $5.65 cleaning charge with a tenacity of a honey badger defending its young. Top institutional investors take after his "not a penny more" philosophy with pride. After 2008, investors took advantage of funds' need for LP money to push through a fee reduction. Then the huge market recovery came about in 2009 and funds became hot again. They saw their chance and raised fees again. So the battle continues on.

***

A peripheral question. As I mentioned above, the smaller hedge funds tend to do better performance-wise than the large funds. Their management fees are not enough to keep the doors open so they have to make good returns and take those incentive fees, creating a sort of Darwinian eat-what-they-cook situation. And it is just easier to invest a tiny fund (again, just ask Warren Buffett). **Many people would then wonder: If it is so much easier to invest with smaller amounts of money then why not simply invest in many small hedge funds rather than one huge one?**

This solution is not so simple. SEC regulations used to make it illegal for hedge funds to advertise their services to common folk like you or me (Look below to learn more about what is changing and what it might do to the industry). People who get to invest in hedge funds have to hit certain income or wealth thresholds. Faced with the possibility that any sort of marketing can be misconstrued as the illegal mass-consumer kind, smaller funds often choose to simply forgo it. Their investors come by personal contacts and word-of-mouth recommendation. So the first problem many LPs face is just <u>finding</u> these diamonds in the rough and then <u>establishing a close enough relationship</u> with them to make them want to take the money. This lack of transparency makes it hard to compare different hedge funds - something very different from how it is in the mutual fund industry.

(Many of the fund marketing rules we talked about in the above are changing with the passage of the JOBS act, which makes it legal for small investment funds to advertise. It still bars them though from taking money from the ordinary masses like you and me. This makes it very interesting for some hedge funds who want to grow larger. Should they build an advertising strategy? Does it make sense to start putting themselves out there or is it just going to subject them to more scrutiny? Right now, the implications are far off and the SEC has yet to formalize what is right or wrong. So it is too early to say.)

Also as you will find in the next section, many LPs are not industry fat cats with a mere couple million dollars to invest. **They are often massive professional organizations who have many millions - sometimes billions - allocated for investment in hedge funds.** While the large hedge funds may not have the same return profile as their smaller counterparts, they do have a proven record in handling those huge figures. They equip their infrastructure with the proper checks, balances and anti-fraud procedures to make sure that the money is not going to get mysteriously whisked away to some Swiss bank account. The only thing worse than getting mediocre returns on a large amount of money is getting <u>defrauded</u> on a large amount of money.

Not only do these organizations have to invest a lot of money, they are not always heavily staffed, with many repercussions. A fund has to be "due diligenced" which means it has to be put through a series of inspections and investigations to make sure the proper anti-fraud and corporate governance procedures are implemented. These are often conducted through questionnaires called Requests for Information. They are a real doozy to handle - many dozens of pages long and stuffed to the brim with single-spaced legalese dealing with things such as the history of the firm, the firm's ownership, investment procedures, conflict resolution, and much more. Then there are the reference checks that must be run on the managers (the same kind that an apartment landlord would run on a prospective tenant). All of these must be done regardless of the fund's size.

Due diligence is time consuming. So if an LP can do these procedures for just one big fund instead of many tiny ones, then that avoids a logistics nightmare. **A large fund can smooth the process along by hiring dedicated investor relations and fund marketing staff to answer due diligence questions and address relevant issues.** I worked with people on this side of the business and the sheer amount of required client service - answering questions and addressing issues - can get overwhelming. You really need someone giving this their full attention. A portfolio manager of a small fund cannot do that; their hands are full investing. Taking on a big institutional client would probably sink them.

For a large professional investing institution with a financial duty to their stakeholders, no exceptions can be made even if this tiny fund makes 100% every year. Just too risky.

Who Invests in a Hedge Fund?

It is more than just rich people!

Very true that many rich folks invest in these funds. A Bill Gates, Rockefeller or Vanderbilt - all of those big names can be found amongst the clientele. But as I hinted at in the last section, the largest fund LPs are not individuals but institutions - professional organizations set up to manage pools of money. These large organizations can include bodies like pension funds, university endowments, foundation endowments, and foreign investment bodies like sovereign wealth funds. Each of them have their own specific needs and investment guidelines but they all owe a duty to the people who gave them their money to invest with. **They are the asset management community's largest customers.**

This section is as pretty much a list. Not that creative or artful but it helps keep all these investors organized. There are 7 parts to this list - 7 common LP organizations - and they are all listed below so you know to look for them:

~ Pension funds

~ Endowments

~ Sovereign Wealth Funds

~ Banks

~ Insurance companies

~ Family Offices

~ Other Hedge Funds

~ Itself

Of course I would also add "rich individuals" but we already know who those are. I am not going to say that this is all of it or that every organization you can find out there fits neatly into just one of these categories, but it would be hard to do better.

***

<u>Pension funds</u> are set up for a group of people - government employees or teachers for example - and dollars from their paycheck go to the fund. If the labor agreement asks of such, the employers also contribute some amount of money as well. **The pension fund manager then invests that money accordingly so that when those people retire and need income for living and medical costs, the pension fund would have that money in hand.**

Pension funds have it hard: **Contributions from both the employee and employer side are running down and the costs of taking care of the retired, who often live far beyond expectations, are skyrocketing.** Pensions for corporate employees have largely died out as they are replaced with 401Ks and IRAs -

the costs are simply too much. Public pensions do not have the same flexibility. A company failing under the weight of its corporate pension can simply declare bankruptcy and then throw off those obligations in bankruptcy. The provider of a public pension is often a city or state government, which makes the bankruptcy option either untenable or disastrous. The public pensions therefore have this huge mark that they have to hit year after year in order to stay ahead of the big obligations that they need to pay out to their constituents. Not only that, as a steward of other people's money, a pension fund must optimize for the highest investment returns while at the same time fending off political meddling from outsiders as well as the temptation to be a meddler itself.

An example of a pension fund that takes its responsibilities seriously is CalPERS. CalPERS is the largest pension fund in the United States and one of the savviest institutional investors in the world, having delivered above-market returns for the past twenty or so years despite taking a cold bath in 2008. They do it by being incredibly smart and demanding investors. CalPERS commands a fierce respect from the crowd. Government pensions across the country are underfunded to the point of disaster yet CalPERS, despite being the largest pension in the country, remains above-water. CalPERS is known for using its size for its own advantage, pushing for changes as a shareholder to bring more value to its stake. This rock-the-boat behavior is not uncommon with hedge funds (and it is in that section where we will give this strategy more light) but highly unusual for a big institutional investor like a pension fund.

You are going to hear a whole lot more about pension funds so don't worry if some of that stuff I talked about just now did not make any sense to you.

Sovereign wealth funds are set up by a country to invest outside their own country. These funds are often fueled and seeded by the wealth derived from natural resources - the fund for Abu Dhabi and Saudi Arabia are well known (and their investments sometimes cause public hysteria) but there are other large bodies as well. Norway has one of the largest sovereign wealth funds in the world, seeded by their fossil fuel resources. China, through their trade with the United States, has collected a large amount of US dollars ($2.5 trillion and counting). Some of the money has been plowed into US Treasury bonds (to keep the Americans spending money on Chinese goods) but a portion of it has also been used to seed a sovereign wealth fund.

The general goal of having a sovereign wealth fund is to invest a country's financial resources in preparation for the future. Others however argue that the close relationship between government and finance means that the fund can be forced into spending money for government reasons. A portion of China's sovereign wealth fund - named China Investment Corporation, Ltd - has been used to invest in China's state-owned banks, African infrastructure ventures, and other foreign resources. Because the fund is intimately tied to the government leadership, it can be hard to keep politics from meddling with investment decisions.

Endowments are run by both nonprofit foundations and universities but they share the same goal: To provide for their benefactors a future stream of payments so that foundation goals may be met. Harvard University has the largest university endowment in the world with over $30 billion while the Bill and Melinda Gates Foundation has a titanic endowment even larger than that. **Money for endowments go to pay these organizations' expenses and gifts - scholarships, charitable grants, or just paying the bills.** These organizations are often required by law to pay a certain percentage of assets to retain their qualification as a nonprofit so as custodians they must keep this requirement in mind.

Banks also occasionally appear on LP rolls. Large retail banks that take in deposits from everyday folks have to pay interest on those deposits, especially if they are held in savings accounts that yield some amount of interest. Often times these banks would fund these payments through the interest revenue that they collect on mortgages, credit cards, and small business loans that they make to customers. However, if the deposit base is large enough a bank can also make private equity and hedge fund investments to diversify their portfolios and squeeze some more profit for the books.

Insurance companies also occasionally invest in hedge funds and private equity. Why do they need to? When you buy insurance, you pay a monthly stream of premiums to the insurance company and they collect these premiums from a large group of people in the event that some calamity happens and those people need the money. The money has to be there when the calamity happens, so most insurance companies don't go out and do stuff willy-nilly but the laws and regulations do allow the companies to invest a certain part of it into risky assets beyond just the plain treasury bond and savings account. Any investment gains above and beyond the amount required to be returned to the insured claimants is pure profit for the insurance company. Many of these insurance companies still invest in nothing riskier than Treasury bonds - mostly because there is always the risk that some catastrophe could come along and force them to disburse that money very quickly - but a few more adventurous types take a chunk of that money and invest it into hedge funds and private equity funds to get that extra bit of return.

Reinsurance companies also fall under this category. What are they? Reinsurance companies are companies that insure other insurance companies. Does that make sense? Sometimes there are risks just too big for a single insurance company to take on. For example, a company might underwrite an insurance policy for a very risky tornado zone. Because the company deems it likely that at some point in time during the insurance contract's there is going to be a big tornado, it might choose to try and "water down" the risk it took on by spreading it amongst a bunch of other insurance companies. So instead of just 1 company getting the premiums from the tornado-stricken policy-holders, it is a bunch. This way if a tornado comes along then it is not just that one company which is on the hook. The types of companies that work with the tornado policy-writer (for a fee of course) are called reinsurance companies. Here is the interesting bit: Some of the smartest hedge fund managers start their own reinsurance companies in Bermuda or some other tax haven, start taking on policies from other insurers, and invest all that policy money into the hedge fund manager's fund. David Einhorn's Greenlight Capital has a reinsurance arm and it is publicly traded under the ticker symbol GLRE. Steve Cohen's SAC Capital has one too. The reason for this is not because David Einhorn and Steve Cohen has suddenly realized that they can do reinsurance too. The reinsurance business is actually run at breakeven or a tiny bit of loss. What they realize is that having this reinsurance company is like having a LP at your side who you can count on in keep their money invested with your fund even if there is extreme choppiness in the markets. As you will see later, this is very important to delivering good returns.

Family offices are small companies set up by extremely wealthy families or individuals with the sole purpose of managing just that family or individual's money. For example, Cascade Investments is a firm set up to manage Bill Gates' wealth. MSD Capital is a private family office set up to manage Michael Dell's money (yes that Dell of Dell Computers). This setup eliminates a lot of potential conflicts in interest between the asset manager and the asset owner. Anyone owning south of maybe $100 million or so should not bother so it is reserved for the ultra-wealthy. For example, MSD Capital has under management some $14 billion spread out over all kinds of assets including real estate and private companies. Michael Dell first seeded MSD Capital back in 1998 with $400 million of his own money. It turned out to be an incredibly astute move. In other words, that is what it took just to get the company off the ground.

Some hedge and private equity funds have other funds as clients. Sometimes if a talented portfolio manager wants to run his own fund his former bosses would start him off with a seed investment. This is usually called a subadvisor arrangement and it helps both parties. The old fund gets to keep the man's talents and the new fund is off and running right away. Other funds exclusively invest in other hedge funds, offering their LPs the benefit of access and diversification. Access because the best hedge funds do not advertise and generally do not often take on new investors. Diversification because different managers supposedly have different styles. The fee on fee structure of these

33

fund-of-funds (as they are called) curtailed the field's growth after 2008 delivered some terrible returns.

And lastly, many hedge funds and private equity funds invest in themselves. In the last section I talked about how years of great performance can result in the fund manager becoming his own biggest investor. Also, many funds set up pools of employee capital where accountants, secretaries, operating staff, and other mere mortals can invest in a fund. This can be done despite the employees not meeting the SEC required regulations because the employees are insiders. The intent is obvious: Funds and their employees should be incentivized to do their best. Such a thing happens when they know that their own money is in the fund they are managing.

Often when a fund becomes so successful and its managers get paid so much, the people investing in the funds are all the same people managing the investments. I mentioned this earlier. Some of the funds in this category include the most successful funds ever created in the hedge fund world: Quantum (George Soros), Medallion (James Simons and Renaissance Technologies), and Bridgewater (Ray Dalio).

The best thing about running your own money is that you are totally in control. You know your own investments. This not only means that you are well motivated to win, but also that you are going to stick with what you have. Earlier, I mentioned that John Paulson has been having a terrible last few years. Most funds that have −40% performance would be really worried about their own survival. Paulson is not because pretty much the whole fund is made up of his and his employees' money.

Even if all the pension funds and sovereign wealth funds leave, Paulson's funds will march on because it is he who is in control. That is a great thing to be able to have.

***

Oh my gosh, so what just happened?! It must have seemed like I ran through this so fast. Perhaps you got a bit left behind back there in the weeds? Fear not, I am heading back in to get you!

~ **Pension funds** - Funds contributed by workers so that they can secure money for their retirement; they are having a tough time nowadays

~ **Endowments** - Funds owned by non profit organizations so that they can afford to do their work

~ **Sovereign wealth funds** - Big funds set up by governments to invest. A lot of the big ones are oil fueled

~ **Banks** - They need to get extra money to pay interest or to keep as profit and investing in these funds help get that

~ **Insurance Companies** - Similar to banks, they are looking for diversification on the funds that they hold for themselves

~ **Family offices** - Very rich people setting up their **own** companies to look after their very rich assets

~ **Other funds** - Other hedge funds or private equity funds. Very incestuous eh?

~ **Itself** - Managers have to make sure that the food they serve has to be good because they are for sure going to be eating it!

Together, these are the biggest asset management organizations in the world. In 2013, they held a total of $117 trillion. Below is a chart on the breakdown of who holds what. You might be surprised to find so much invested in pensions and insurance companies.

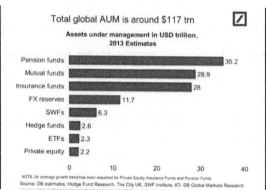

Regardless of who is holding the money, what they have to do with it is clear: Invest it for proper returns in the future.

Why Do People Give Money to Hedge/Private Equity Funds?

Was it not because of the nice suits and the caviar lunches?

Over time institutional investors - and especially pension funds - find themselves leaning heavier and heavier on hedge funds and private equity. Let us take a look at some data.

Look here at the table below, which was published mid-October 2011 by the magazine Pensions & Investments:

Fund	One-year return	Bench-mark	Outper-formance vs. benchmark (basis points)	Total hedge fund assets ▲	% of total fund assets	One-year growth of hedge fund assets	% of hedge fund assets directly invested	% of hedge fund assets in funds of funds
South Carolina Retirement	11.6%	4.2%	740	$5,566	21.2%	13.8%	41.0%	59.0%
PennPSERS	13.2%	8.0%	520	$5,300	10.3%	3.3%	100.0%	0
CalPERS	6.6%	5.7%	90	$5,300	2.2%	-3.6%	70.0%	30.0%
Missouri Public Schools*	16.8%	16.3%	52	$4,244	13.8%	57.1%	100.0%	0
Texas Teachers	5.9%	2.3%	360	$4,158	3.8%	4.0%	83.0%	17.0%
N.J. Division of Investment	10.7%	6.3%	437	$3,902	5.3%	11.5%	63.3%	36.7%
MassPRIM	7.5%	5.0%	255	$3,600	7.2%	12.5%	0	100.0%
Texas County & District	9.4%	6.7%	271	$3,415	18.6%	19.1%	100.0%	0
PennSERS	7.6%	3.3%	430	$2,800	10.6%	-40.1%	0	100.0%
Missouri State Employees	11.1%	4.1%	696	$2,067	27.0%	21.6%	73.0%	26.3%
Illinois Teachers	12.4%	4.2%	821	$1,486	4.0%	23.3%	32.4%	67.6%
Ohio School Employees	11.4%	6.7%	473	$1,372	12.9%	48.3%	100.0%	0
W.Va. Investment Mgmt. Board	7.8%	4.7%	311	$851	8.4%	-1.2%	100.0%	0
Total				$44,061				
Averages	10.3%	6.1%	420		11.2%	13.0%		
HFR Fund Weighted Composite	11.5%							
HFR Fund of Funds Composite	6.7%							

Pensions & Investments Online Oct 17, 2011[3]

Just in case you have trouble reading through that graphic, let me walk you through some of the more interesting data points.

There are 13 pension funds on the table and as a whole, they are looking to put $44 billion into hedge funds. Some of these pension funds have been dedicating a very large part of their portfolios to this risky asset class. Texas County & District is investing 18.6% of their total fund assets into hedge funds. South Carolina Retirement, 21.2%. Missouri State Employees, an astounding 27%! In comparison, when you as a person dedicate 5% or more of your portfolio to a single investment then the fate of your portfolio becomes very closely intertwined with that particular something. And some of these funds are investing a full 20% and more!

If you expand beyond just hedge funds to include private equity (what we would call "alternative investments") then the allocations start getting ever so more intense. Below are the fair values of every asset owned by the Washington State Investment Board ("WSIB"), a pension fund for Washington state employees and a pioneering partner in private equity with Kohlberg Kravis and Roberts ("KKR").

[3] You can go play with this interactive graphic at the following URL:

http://www.pionline.com/article/20111017/CHART02/111019907/table-public-pension-plan-hedge-fund-portfolios

Investment Type	Total Fair Value
Asset Backed Securities	$ 188,397,863
Residential Mortgage Backed Securities	2,875,073,669
Commercial Mortgage Backed Securities	478,293,349
Corporate Bonds Domestic (USD)	1,624,171,354
Corporate Bonds Foreign (USD)	4,405,322,481
Corporate Bonds Foreign (Non USD)	666,548,150
US Government Treasuries	673,678,191
Treasury Inflation Protected Securities (TIPS)	847,259,298
Total Retirement Funds Investment Categorized	11,758,744,355
Investments Not Required to be Categorized	
Commingled Equity Index Funds	10,204,805,721
Corporate Stock - U.S. Dollar Denominated	659,329,617
Corporate Stock - Non U.S. Dollar Denominated	7,504,393,760
Alternative Investments	21,654,098,699
Liquidity	1,061,656,998
Total Investments Not Categorized	41,084,284,795
Total Investments	$ 52,843,029,150

Courtesy of the WSIB 2010 Annual Report

The total value of everything in WSIB's fund is $52.8 billion. Of that entire portfolio, alternative investments - private equity and hedge funds - make up $21.7 billion. So about 41% of the entire pension fund. Your fund and the thousands of pensioners depending on your fund will live or die by how that 41% does.

***

Lots of charts and a lot of diagrams. What does it all mean? Pension funds are giving a lot of money to private equity and hedge funds. So why is this the case? There are a few instinctive reasons as well as broad trends behind this move. I want to focus on two.

1) Investment institutions are taking on heavier burdens. They need more money to pay their pensioners.

2) The popularization of the Yale Model.

In the next few sections, we will talk a little bit about these two big trends and if what the pension funds are doing actually work. We also look at an alternative approach to institutional investing, pioneered by one of the largest sovereign wealth funds in the world - Norway.

Concept: Diversification and Asset Classes

In this section, we are taking a look at two big concepts. First is the idea of asset classes. The second is about diversification. If you want to skip over this section here and just move on then feel free to just read this "too long didn't read" version: An asset class is a grouping assigned to a number of items that perform differently in the market from other asset classes. Diversification says that you should never put all your eggs in one basket. So that's everything in just a few sentences. Want to know more? Then keep on reading.

***

Asset Classes

The investable world has been split up in into buckets called asset classes. The usual divisions are natural resource assets (gold, oil, and timber), absolute return (arbitrage and other unusual circumstances), private equity (including venture capital), and stocks/bonds. (Note: You will learn about a lot of these later on in the book so do not fear if you just got confused.)

These asset classes often have different physical characteristics from each other but in general the manner in which they are grouped is determined by their assumed risk and return profile. There is also occasionally some discussion around whether or not a certain asset deserves to be put into its own class. There is no central authority making a decision on this so the interpretation is up in the air. Sometimes people argue that gold is an asset class all of its own because of its unique historical role as a replacement for currency. I have heard that Apple stock should be seen as its own asset class because it is very uncorrelated with the rest of the stock market! So the word "asset class" is very much about grey zones. If someone offers the claim that such and such belongs to its own special asset class, treat it with suspicion.

Diversification

The theory has long been that in order to reduce risk in your portfolio, your portfolio must reflect the "market". This is because they identified two types of risk in the world: Risk in the "market" which you **can never** avoid and risk in an individual "thing in the market" which you **can** avoid by investing as many "things in the market" as you can. You may be surprised to find, however, that financial theorists define the market as being made up of things beyond just stocks and bonds. **In fact according to theory, the market also includes works of art, timber forests, rare minerals and even Antarctic ice.** Everything with a price is part of this nebulous "market." Of course not all of it can be traded like stocks. That fact however has not stopped people from trying to use complex mathematics to create the next new financial instruments. There was a recent dustup between movie studios and investors when a financial firm tried to trade on the box office revenues of movies.

So the theory dictates that in order to keep portfolio assets as safe and stable as possible, large institutional investors need to diversify into investments outside the normal realm. That is basically the practical advice on top of that "risk" and "market" mumbo jumbo. **Imagine purchasing a timber forest.** People will see a stock or bond as being fundamentally different from an item such as a timber forest. Therefore, these people - and the market - will value it differently. A potential buyer figures out the price to a timber forest not by going to the stock market but by Googling recent sales of similar timber forests. Therefore, the prices for timber forests do not crash when stock prices crash. This way when the stock markets melt down - and they always will - your pension is not ruined.

The institution evaluates all the possible asset classes and decides how much they are going to invest in each bucket. If they feel like the asset class is going to be a winner the next couple of years, they "overweight" it. This means they add more of it to their portfolio. If they feel otherwise, then they "underweight" it, buying a smaller amount for their portfolio. **Note: Even if they decide to underweight something, there is no instance where they put no money in a bucket.** Every bucket must have something - for diversification's sake and in case their research is wrong.

I am not saying it is a better idea to hold forests instead of stocks. The answer according to the professors, is to hold both. Suppose a fire hits your timber forest, the value of your timber plummets but your stock portfolio will not. **When you hold many different types of assets, it is very unlikely that all of them are dropping in price at the same time.** When one is going down another is likely to be going up or staying where it is. Your portfolio takes a hit but dodges a total catastrophe. Take a look at one pension fund: the San Diego Employees Retirement Association (SDCERA). In 2005, SDCERA made the ill-fortuned decision to invest in a hedge fund called Amaranth Advisors, a very big $9 billion hedge fund that collapsed in 2006 and practically lost everything[4]. SDCERA itself lost $100 million as part of the debacle. Despite this massive loss - the biggest hedge fund collapses ever - SDCERA returned 14.57% that year, a very good return.

You would be surprised at what people can invest in to make a buck. Some invest in unique works of art. Others work with oil companies to build oil rigs. And some finance movies. Relativity Media brings Wall Street money to Hollywood, funding movies like *300*, *The Social Network*, and *The Fast & Furious*.[5]

The institutional investor sees the hedge fund and private equity fund as part of a specific asset class. This is because of the claim that fund managers can deliver returns uncorrelated to the rest of the market. Thus, the investor makes an allocation to this asset class. With many hundreds of institutional investors managing many trillions of dollars, the tiny percentage allocations add up into hundreds of billions of dollars. That's a whole lot of money.

***

The financial crisis in 2008 turned a lot of these risk-return concepts on their head. When the crisis started, LPs wanted their money back and the withdrawal orders came in by the dozens. However funds found that they could not give back what they promised because the prices in their portfolios were moving down so quickly. What was

---

[4] In September 2006, Amaranth lost $6.4 billion on natural gas futures. What does that mean? Basically a trader thought that the price of natural gas would rise by a great amount in the coming winter and bet a whole lot of money on it. It did not and Amaranth had to close down.

[5] You would be impressed by the money-making machine that Hollywood is. They run laps around ultra-smart Wall Street people. Read Edward Jay Epstein's The Hollywood Economist for some interesting stories.

listed as a $1 million dollar investment on your hedge fund account statement shrank to $600,000.

While there are probably a million different reasons for this, here's one way to think about what happened then: You can attribute a lot of this to the way that people value some of these portfolio assets. The generally accepted way to do it is to look up the prices of its peers. What happened is that when everyone is looking to convert their assets to cash and pull that cash out of the financial system, prices fall like a rock on every item in the market, including those outside just the stock and bond market.

In crises like these, you should rely on the steady nature of your non stock and bond assets to bolster the rest of the portfolio. These would include your hedge funds and private equity funds. What investors found though was that their hedge funds were investing in financial instruments like stocks and bonds. No matter the manager's individual skill, the stock lost money. In fact, since the 90s, correlations between stocks and funds have been rising:

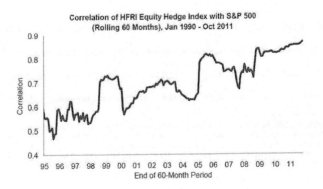

Correlation of HFRI Equity Hedge Index with S&P 500
(Rolling 60 Months), Jan 1990 - Oct 2011

This chart, which comes out of a Morgan Stanley research note issued November 2011, tracks the correlation between a bundle of hedge funds and the plain old S&P 500. The higher the correlation (meaning the closer it gets to 1.0), the closer they move in lock-step direction. At this chart's most recent (Oct 2011), the correlation is at 0.9, which means in all practicality when the S&P 500 goes up, the hedge funds go up. And when the S&P 500 goes down, the hedgies go down too. So investors losing money on their own private portfolios in bad markets looked to their fancy hedge funds for comfort only to find that their hedge fund accounts were at times doing **even worse** (Because some of these hedge funds were using leverage to amplify their returns. This leverage caused the losses to be that much greater). Great diversification that was. Investors are paying huge fees to managers to insulate themselves from the market. If there is such a high correlation, what are these investors paying for?

Likewise with private equity. Investors who looked at private equity funds then saw that though the companies were private, managers pegged the value of their investments by looking at similar companies in the public market. As all of those are doing terribly, the same then can be said about the private equity companies as well. Ergo, private equity fund portfolios lost value too.

Alternative asset management firms like hedge funds and private equity won a place as a separate asset class because they claim to be able to deliver returns uncorrelated returns. What many investors found was that for most of these firms, their returns were very correlated indeed. **Eventually, every economic asset has to be valued, and the best way to do that is to find a market.** Funds bought from the market and sold into the market. **During a massive financial crisis like the one in 2008, the toppling of one market - subprime bonds - led to the fall of the rest, so the value of every asset in the portfolio that could possibly be sold in the market crashed hard with titanic consequences.** As a result, virtually every investable asset in the world moved in tight correlation with each other. From 2007 to 2009 (the "Great Recession"), it was found that stocks of all sizes from small cap to large cap were strongly linearly correlated with one another. The correlation between Small cap and large cap stocks were 0.95 (with 1.0 being that they were 100% perfectly correlated in the same direction). Large cap with medium cap? 0.97. Even emerging market and international stocks moved in lockstep with one another. Basically the only thing that did not move in the same direction were Treasurys, which was the best performing asset that you could have had during the Financial Crisis.

As the Euro-zone debt crisis took hold in the financial markets in the second half of 2011, people noticed that everything in the market started moving in the same direction no matter what the "asset class" they belonged to. The WSJ reported in Dec 20, 2011 that *every* hedge fund strategy - macro, activist, event-driven (you will learn more about these later on) lost money. An index tracking the performance of all hedge funds lost 8% for the year, which is worse than how mutual funds did in 2011.[6] The hedge funds did not hedge well enough, it appears.

---

[6] You can read more about this from the WSJ though it is behind the subscriber paywall: http://online.wsj.com/article/BT-CO-20111219-709507.html

Two Trends

Before we talked about asset classes, I pointed out two big trends in pension funds and institutional investing driving the big boom in hedge funds and private equity funds. They were:

1) Investment institutions are taking on heavier burdens. They need more money to pay their pensioners.

2) The popularization of the Yale Model.

Let's go into some more detail, shall we?

***

1) Investment institutions are taking on heavier burdens. They need more money to pay their pensioners.

Let's start with the first bit. You probably do not need to be reminded that there is a recession going on. Times are tough and things are no different for the institutional investors, especially the pension funds. Like I said, the pension funds could be having better days. Contributions from the employee and employer sides are falling and the costs they need to pay out are rising from year to year. **They have large amounts of money but it is getting harder and harder to make anything more than a tiny bit out of it because interest rates are so low.** State and city governments are going bankrupt so they are not going to be able to help these funds.

48

Pension fund accounting involves some of the most convoluted and ridiculous assumptions in all of accounting. It basically works kind of like this. A pension fund has obligations - cash or health services going to pensioners - that it needs to pay and assets to pay those obligations. If the obligation is higher than the assets then they somehow have to make up for the shortcoming. Either someone - the company or organization maintaining the pension - contributes more or the pensioners get less overall benefits from the fund. However the way by which they calculate the obligations and assets is much more complicated than just a simple sum. There is discounting involved ... and division ... and other math. **The assumptions make more of a difference than how the discount is calculated.** For example, if you assume that the fund can sustainably invest and grow assets at 8% then yes of course then it can make up for all of its obligations. Unfortunately, hitting that number is easier said than done.

2) The popularization of the Yale Model.

David Swensen is probably one of the most influential people in investing history. He has been the manager of the Yale Endowment Fund for many years now, overseeing over $20 billion in assets. This is a big gain from just 20 years ago, when the fund stood at just $2.8 billion. The fund has done very well too. In the 10 years since June 30, 2012, the endowment has had annual returns of roughly 10% while stocks have 6% and bonds 5.6%. Does not seem like a whole much that 4% but it actually does matter.

In his book *Pioneering Portfolio Management*, Swensen talked about how a fund should invest its money. In short, he argued that since funds had a very long term outlook that they should not be investing in things that are easily tradeable on the

49

markets. **That means that an endowment like Yale's should stay away from public stocks like Apple or Ford. Instead, they should buy really unusual things that are hard to find a market for but as a result give you a much higher return.** A good example is real estate. A house does not get sold often but when it does the seller might get a great return on it. The risk with owning a piece of real estate is that if things go south in a hurry and you need to raise money now then it gets really hard to raise the money by selling your real estate. This inability to sell quickly is called illiquidity and we will discuss it more in the future.

Illiquidity normally makes investors really nervous. After all, people value the ability to raise cash on a dime right? Well, Swensen says that endowments should go the opposite route. They should take advantage of that nervousness. Endowments and other institutional investors should not mind being unable to raise cash quickly because if they do not need to. They need to pay for certain things on a consistent basis that can be planned for way ahead of schedule.

Results matter and Yale's has been impressive enough such that its model has been adopted by endowments and other funds all around the world. This is in part why WSIB and other pension funds dedicate so much money to private equity and other alternative asset managers. Institutional investors actually like that these hedge funds and private equity funds invest in unusual things. **They like that private equity funds lock up money for a long time because they can wait a long time to get it back and arguably it would come back with a much higher return**. And that higher return is something that these institutional investors definitely need.

Does the Yale Model work? Hard to say. While Yale's long term results cannot be argued against, it has been tough to replicate. Just look at the whole bevy of endowments and pensions underperforming across the country. Over the past 5 years, data compiled by the National Association of College and University Business Officers found that college endowments returned just 1.1% annually after fees (as of June 2012). That's like nothing. A simple 60/40 portfolio (60% stocks, 40% bonds) would have done twice as better. The financial crisis in 2008 really wiped out a lot of endowments and forced them to reevaluate the strategy. If your illiquid investments are just as crappy as the liquid ones then why bother to buy them? A report published by the Center for Social Philosophy and the Tellus Institute looked at 6 endowments in New England and concluded that the Yale Model underestimated the risks involved and jeopardized endowment income. A lot of studies and analyses (including those done by Swensen himself) have found that the majority of the Yale model's greater returns come not from hedge funds, stocks, bonds, lumber or whatever but the huge expose to private equity funds. Not just KKR and buyout type private equity either, mostly venture capital funds benefitting from the glory days of the dotcom boom.

I am not really in any position to tell you whether or not the Yale Model should be adopted or whether it should be dropped. That is out of the scope of this work. My goal is just to get you familiarized with what it means as well as present any big alternatives. One in particular operates across the Atlantic in the frigid waters of Scandinavia.

The Norway Model. The Yale Model.

Earlier, we talked about how many big asset management institutions - pension funds like CalPERS - diversify their risk by purchasing and holding different "classes" of investment assets. Theory holds that since these assets belong to their own individual classes, their prices will go up or down at different times. If you own forest timber, its price fluctuations differ from that of Apple stock.

Then we talked a bit about the Yale model, which says that endowments should take on some illiquidity risks for the long term so that they can get higher than average returns. The popularization of this model plus a need for higher returns from funds meant that soon everyone was investing in random things like timber forests and oil rigs. Well now we are going to present a different investment model for big institutional investors: the Norway Model.

Most people confuse Norway with Sweden. I do it all the time. And even the most well read people tend to think of Norway only as the country that awards the Nobel Peace Prize. However, Norway is also one of the richest countries in the world. Part of this can be attributed to sheer luck but a good part of it stems from disciplined financial management and the second largest sovereign wealth fund in the world.

First of all, let's start from the beginning. Norway is lucky in that its land sits on a crapload of oil that it does not need. Hydropower dams power all their infrastructure and cities. So they get to sell their oil into the open market, which has brought huge sums of money into the country's coffers. Most countries with oil and other great natural resources take all this money and waste it on corruption and pleasing the immediate masses - something that is called the "resource curse"[7]. Norway avoided that and put the windfall gains from their oil sales into a separately run sovereign wealth fund. Today, the fund is worth some $650 billion and is one of the largest SWFs in the world[8]. Every year it sends some money to the Norwegian government to help pay for expenses and cover any deficits.

Norway's SWF is one of the most transparent and well-run in the world. If you go to their website (http://www.nbim.no/) you will find that the site has displayed very prominently a little tickers that shows the fund's value at that exact period of time. Any day you can download their annual report and see what stocks they are holding. They do not invest in the stocks of companies it considers to be unethical. It cannot invest inside the country (so to avoid the taint of corruption) and it has one simple goal: Make 4% a year.

Fund market value in NOK*

3 722 675 375 078

→ More on the fund's size

On the website, it moves

[7] Should read about it. It's real interesting. There are a lot of countries suffering nowadays because of it: http://en.wikipedia.org/wiki/Resource_curse
[8] You can debate on whether or not it is the largest. Japan has a massive pension fund that is much larger at some $1.5 trillion. However, it is not professionally run. Abu Dhabi has a fund too but its size is not known.

While the Yale model embraces illiquidity and unusual assets, Norway runs its fund in almost the exact opposite way. It largely invests in just stocks and bonds with a tiny little bit in real estate. Right now it is about 60% in stocks and 40% in bonds. The majority of its stocks are in the US with the rest in Europe. They own shares in 9,000 companies and holds about 1% of every significant stock on the earth. They hire some external fund managers to pick stocks for them but not a lot. Recently, they took 5% out of bonds and put it into real estate, most of it in the United States and Europe.

Wow, that was really simple to explain.

In 2011 a paper came out by a few academics arguing that the Norway Model is a legitimate competitor model for other endowments to follow. Its simplicity and transparency for one thing is certainly something to admire. Many funds are nowhere as open as the Norwegian SWF are. In fact recently people had to sue CalPERS to release information about how well its venture capital funds do. This is not money that belongs to a private family. This money belongs to thousands of individuals who have little insight into what is going on with their investments!

But the Norway Model has its own problems too. For one thing it is hardly "asset management". Active stock pickers manage less than 10% of the total fund. Thus it seems like the fund is just a huge passive index replicating the larger stock market. The fund's employees argue that this is not the case, but it appears to be so. This means that the fund is very much exposed to the vagaries of the market, as the country found out in

2008 when the fund lost 23% of its value. Some people would argue the pension fund is leaving money on the table that can be gained by active management or alternative investments as espoused by the Yale model. But that too seems to be up for debate especially when you take into consideration the difficulties associated with (successfully) implementing the Yale model and active management's frequent inability to keep up with the market over the long term. Norway's simplicity and success has started to attract attention. In March 2013 CalPERS has started to reexamine its own active management philosophies with a consideration of a partial move to the passive management Norway espouses. There is a lot to like in the Norway Model, but if endowments were to adopt it then that would put a lot of fund managers out of business. Hedge funds, private equity funds, and other alternative asset management firms employ thousands of people. The entire fund of Norway employs just 300 people to execute its simple strategy.

With the prices of oil remaining at high levels, Norway will continue to deposit huge sums of money into its fund. Those sums will in turn be reinvested into the financial markets. According to the Financial Times, the fund is expected to have more than a trillion dollars within the next ten years. It is interesting to contrast the Norwegians' (who by the way are socialists) growing excess surplus with the Americans' growing debt. Actually scratch that. Scratch that, not interesting. Just depressing.

***

Here arrives the end of the "Starting Off" material. To be honest, if you have read through this and grasped a good percentage of what I had to say then you are already far ahead of the majority of the people in the population. But rather than stop here, why not go a little bit further?

I must warn you that the material that you are about to start on hits harder and faster than what we just went through. I am going to assume that you have read this prerequisite material already. I am going to do my best but there may still be times when this stuff starts to feel like a bit of a drag. If you do find this to be the case, then skip around until something *does* catch your interest. Learning is about being engaged and hooked on what you are learning. Once the time is right and your knowledge base is strong enough, you can always come back to the skipped stuff later.

For those reading in order the next section is on event-driven and sidepocket investing. I hope you find it interesting.

Hedge Fund Strategies

There are piranhas in the stock market waters.

There are hundreds of hedge funds out there working 24/7 to make money for their investors. The first question many people might ask then is this: "How are they going about trying to do it?" (And perhaps a second question to follow up is: "Can I do it too?"). The interesting thing is that they are not just buying and selling things willy-nilly. Many of these funds practice a certain set of investment strategies or work on a foundation of investment philosophies that we can call package up and call a "style". Furthermore, what is cool is that these hedge fund investing styles, like the autumn and spring looks on the fashion catwalk, come in and out of vogue from year to year. That means that in a particular year, one style might really kill it in the market and make a huge return for its investors but then suddenly fizzle out the next year. There are many reasons for why that might happen. If a hedge fund style is not working that particular season, then it can really hurt the funds that are running it. Below is a great graphic that gives you a sense of the diversity of styles and investing strategies in the hedge fund world:

(Courtesy of Boomerang Capital, who has archived all of their tables over time here[9])

It is kind of amazing when you look at this chart and imagine that for each square there are dozens of individual hedge funds making their living using strategies derived from their niche. It goes to show you that there are many ways that people can make money and beat the market. It just so happens that those ways differ from year to year!

If you examine the table much more closely, the names of the strategies themselves may confuse you. Though of these styles you will recognize from what I have already told you, a lot others will definitely not click at first glance. For example, Global Macro (the green tiles) was the top performing hedge fund investing style in 2010 and 2011 (with 13.5% in 2010 and 6.4% in 2011). Others like Risk Arb or Multi-Strat we will get to in a coming chapter.

---

[9] http://www.boomcap.com/periodicTable.htm

In this section, we are going to take a whirlwind tour through some of the strategies that hedge funds use to generate "alpha" for their investors. Some of these funds use many of these strategies while others specialize in just one or two. For each and every strategy there is a sort of "flagship" hedge fund that most prominently exhibits itself as using such a strategy. My goal for you is that by the end of the chapter you will be much more familiar with what these otherwise-esoteric terms mean in a broad sense. In no way am I going to try to explain how these strategies are going to be executed in a trade-by-trade sense because that is beyond the scope of this book. That being said, I think it is still pretty interesting.

The strategies that we are going to be talking about in the following sub-sections are:

- **Event-driving Investing-Trading** - Taking advantage of how certain events (or catalysts) can predictably affect the market to make good short-term investments

- **Activist Investing** - Making yourself the catalyst by going public with your investment thesis or otherwise somehow agitating the company to make the changes you want to happen

- **Private Placements** - Making investments outside of the public market. Buying certain stocks that are not easily available

- **Arbitrage** - Taking advantage of natural mispricings in the market to make money

- **Momentum Investing** - Taking advantage of human psychological failings to ride a winner higher and higher

- **Global Macro Investing** - Using a philosophy of how the markets will react to broad, worldwide events to make successful investments

A note about what you will learn in this chapter. I would not recommend that you use these strategies in real life, especially if you base your investing off what you read here! These are managers who are not working alone. They have a lot of people working for them, spending 24/7 to assemble the expertise and knowledge make the strategy work. There is a lot of nuance and the purpose of this book is, again, to give you that 10,000-foot aerial view. So ... don't try this at home kids!

With that being said, let's dive in.

Event-Driven Investing/Trading

A favorite hedge fund investing topic.

Undervalued with a catalyst. Event driven strategy. All great keywords to throw into the fund's marketing materials. What does it mean? At the heart of it, events and catalysts are things you can point to and say, "This will make people want to buy or sell the stock." Like shocks in the status quo, they are turning points that lead to major shifts in the stock price. The key thing is that people know that these events are coming which means that a hedge fund can bet money on it, with it being likely that the investment comes out ahead.

In this little section, I hope to explain to use some of the concepts and ideas behind the events that affect a company's stock price movements and point out some specific examples to help cement the idea in your brain. There are five chapters and they cover the span from investing in stock price splits to investing in central bank announcements. Again, it is not comprehensive of every event ever, but I did try to cover the range of what comes up most often around the water cooler and in the financial news media.

***

Splits and Index Funds

In this event, we are going to look at an unusual company - Warren Buffett's Berkshire Hathaway. In 2010, there occurred a series of events that led to a boost in the company's stock price. The curious thing is that people knew that this event would happen and that it would likely cause the stock price to rise. Yet this rise in the stock price only happened once the event happened.

The company is famous for having two classes of stock: Class A and B. Class A shares cost over $100,000 per share which in turn prompted the creation of Class B shares. The Class B shares themselves soon rose to over $3,000 per share. **Even if normal people heard of Berkshire Hathaway, it became hard to invest in the company because their investments had to be made in portions of $3,000 or $100,000.** Most companies when their stock price gets this high do something called a split, where they essentially "break up" a single share into many shares. A $10,000 share becomes 100 shares of $100 each. Nothing else has happened to the company. The company did not introduce a new product or charge into new markets or do anything else that would make investors want to buy more of the stock. The price of a single share simply went down.

Berkshire has resisted a split for a long time reasoning that since splits do nothing for the shareholders fundamentally it would be a waste to do them. The price just kept on rising. The relatively low number of trades in a single day excluded the company from large index measures like the S&P 500.

It all changed when Berkshire acquired railroad Burlington Northern in late 2009 for some $30 billion. It became clear then that the stock had to be split to properly pay for the purchase. A split for the Class B shares was announced several weeks in advance. **Managers began to bet on the split doing good things for the stock.** Why?

The first reason depends on Berkshire Hathaway's following with retail investors - normal folks like you and me. In a split the Class B shares' nominal price will fall from around $3,000 to around $60. Retail investors who previously could only buy in portions of $3,000 can now buy more. Buffett's homegrown following is strong - and it is likely that the effect can positively move the stock price.

The second reason ties into an increased volume of shares and index funds. After the split the volume of shares traded per day will rise. It is mathematics - instead of just 1 share of $3,000 moving around, there are 50 shares of $60. Again, the same amount of money ... just more shares.

Indices are lists created by companies as proxies for the broad stock market. This is necessary because as I have previously explained, nobody really knows what the "broad market" means. Examples of indices include the S&P 500 and NASDAQ and they choose to add or remove certain stocks from their list based on certain criteria. **Index funds read through these lists and buy stocks in an attempt to copy the list.** Investors then invest into the index fund. This way, retail investors like you and me can invest in the "broad market" without having to waste money buying a whole bunch of different stocks and paying transactions fees for each block of shares you buy. With just 1 purchase, you can buy into a piece of the "market", whatever that may mean to you.

(Here, I want to make clear that the **index** and the **index fund** are different entities. They are not one and the same. An index fund tracks an index. An index is just a list of stocks in some proportion created by some researcher.)

Remember I said that these indices excluded Berkshire Hathaway because it did not meet those criteria, the most important of which involves the number of shares traded everyday. **Now that the price has nominally declined and volume has risen, the S&P 500 and other similar indices can add Berkshire.** This is a big deal because index funds must follow the S&P500 and these indices. Once Berkshire is on the index, the funds - and there are many of them as index funds are very popular - must buy the stock to keep the fund up to date with its index. If you can recall from earlier in this book about how hedge funds work to stay ahead of the institutional investors, this is exactly the type of situation they are looking for: A wave of cash blindly buying in and hurdling the stock price upwards. And as predicted, the stock saw a 20% rise in value after the split happened.[10]

The event was the very picture of a catalyst - something an investor can look at in advance and say, "This will make the price go up."[11] That is why hedge funds pay close attention to events: They are opportunities for profitable investment.

***

---

[10] One question someone might have when looking at this event is: Is it necessary that all these index funds have to purchase at the same time? The answer is that it does not matter. While the timing of these purchases may vary from fund to fund, a stock before it is added to an index is often relatively thinly traded. It does not take a lot of trades were a lot of demand to send the price up.
[11] It also happens to be living proof that the market is inefficient but that is another matter.

IPO Lock-Up Period

An IPO is one of the most notable events in a company's history. It gets a lot of press and buzz within the company and if the company is particularly well-known (like, say Facebook) then the whole community gets excited. Why? First, there is prestige of owning a stake in these companies. It raises your own profile to have a stake in a Facebook or LinkedIn. And second, they might look with envy at the price movements an IPO stock would take on that first day of trading. Sometimes a stock can jump 50 or more percent in a single day. People look at the chart and wish that they were one of the lucky few to have bought the stock right when it came out.

There are a lot of words spent in the press about the disadvantage of being a retail investor during the first phase of an IPO. Though I do not think it has become common knowledge, I do think that by now people are more or less aware that it is virtually impossible for them to "get in on the ground floor" of an IPO. Those shares are reserved for investment bankers and the pension and hedge fund clients they serve. And during those first few hours of the day the company goes public, those parties rapidly trade amongst themselves those shares, bidding up to some ridiculous price before flipping it to the first fool dumb enough to hold on for the "long term". The stock then promptly deflates like a pricked balloon.

This rigged game means a whole lot of attention during those first couple days when people are talking amongst themselves about this new hot stock (and the naysayers at the same time talking it down, publishing the standard news articles about how it is a terrible idea to invest in an IPO). Then the IPO happens and everyone forgets about the company as they move onto the next big thing. That stock however will continue to trade and probably do well for about six months, when it is then very likely to shed a whole lot of money.

This is because of the SEC mandated insider lockup period, which usually runs at about six months. **Former employees and current executives of the company are not allowed to sell shares in their company on the day that it goes public.** No, they must wait. However once that lock up period is over, what often happens is that many of those people sell some portion of their shares and tank the stock price. This event is relatively easy to predict, and many brokerage research analysts note it in their research reports.

In recent years a number of prominent Web companies have gone public. Among those are Zynga, LinkedIn, and Groupon. **Early in their years, they attracted their top talent by offering them a whole lot of stock.** This is fine and normal because startups cannot pay as well as big companies can. It is also good because it means that the workers will work extra hard because they feel that if the company does well and goes public then they can get rich.

However, this usually means that by the time that the company goes public there are a whole lot of employees who want to sell their shares but cannot until the lockup period ends. So what happens once that fateful day comes around? Well ... take a look at the numbers. LinkedIn ended the day down some 2% which does not seem that bad but during the trading day it was down by as much as 7%. All those employees selling into the market has a real bad effect on the stock price.

Company	Ticker	Lockup End Date	Stock Drop on Date
Groupon	GRPN	6/1/2012	9%
LinkedIn	LNKD	11/21/2011	2%
Zynga	ZNGA	5/29/2012	8%

But alas, an exception! While the IPO lockup event frequently means a much lower stock price for some IPO companies, it is not always the case. Here is one prominent example: Yelp. Yes, that Yelp. The one that offers online restaurant reviews. It is public! It IPO'ed in March 2012 at $15 and after that traded in a range of about $14 to $32. **But as the end of the 180-day IPO lockup period approached the stock price began to fall because everyone was worried that newly unlocked shareholders would all dump their shares on the market.** It must have been a huge surprise then when the big day rolled around on August 29, 2012, the stock did not go down at all. Instead, it leapt up by 7.5%!

So what happened? Probably the best explanation goes something like this: As the end of the lockup period approached, funds and investors sold the stock short - which means that they borrowed shares and sold them with the expectation of buying them back later at a lower price. They did this because they anticipated that the end of the lockup period would mean a big drop in the stock price. **However, in this case for whatever reason Yelp's shareholders did not dump their shares into the market.** They just held on to them, perhaps thinking that the company was doing very well (and it was, having recently reported 67% quarterly sales growth) which meant it would be dumb to sell. So the stock price did not drop. Suddenly all the funds realized that what they had expected to happen was not happening and frantically "unwound" their trades, meaning that they went and bought back all their shorted shares to close the trade.

A big IPO is always interesting to follow. There is a lot going on all at once. However, I have always been less interested in what happens on that big IPO day as what happens in the days and months after.

***

Spinoffs

Companies can own other companies, but they do not have to own them forever. A parent company can sell its sub-division to a variety of buyers (you can learn more about the types of buyers - strategic and financial - in a later chapter) or it can do something called a spin-off.

What happens in a spin-off? Let's talk about Company A. Company A owns a number of very profitable subsidiaries, two of which are illustrated in the graphic below:

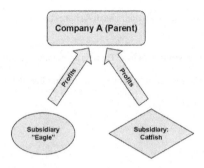

(Yeah, yeah, I know. I'm never going to win a graphic design award)

So you have subsidiary Eagle and subsidiary Catfish. When one company is the subsidiary of another, it means that all the profits of the subsidiary belong to the parent. This is illustrated in the arrows. If the parent wishes, it could demand a dividend paid out from the profits generated by the subsidiary companies.

(How does the parent company "own" its subsidiaries? In the same way that we can "own" a company: By possessing a majority of the subsidiary's common stock. Having over 50% of a company's voting stock means that you can dictate what the company does.)

Now, let's pull back a little bit to get a better perspective. Who owns the parent company? In almost every case, if a company is large enough to own subsidiaries, then the ultimate owners are public shareholders. These are hedge funds, pension funds, and individual investors like you and me buying shares off the market and holding them in stock portfolios. In the graphic below, you can see the total relationship. Profits flow to the parent company which then float the public shareholders (usually in the form of cash dividends):

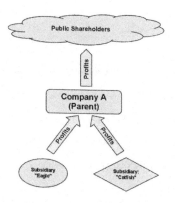

Now let's decide that Company A wants to spin off its Eagle subsidiary to its public shareholders. In practical terms, what happens is that Parent Company A takes all of the shares of the subsidiary and "gives" them to the same shareholders that possess its own shares. Now, the public shareholders who hold the shares of one company - Company A - have the shares of TWO companies: That of Company A and the Eagle subsidiary. This new relationship is illustrated in the graphic below:

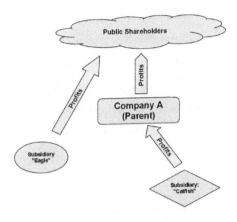

So here's the end result of the spinoff. One company becomes two companies. The individual shareholder who before had some number of one type of share now has some number of two types of shares. Note that Company A now has nothing to do with its former subsidiary. If all of the Eagle subsidiary's shares were spun off, then Company A has no say in how the Eagle subsidiary runs its business.

What kind of subsidiaries are suitable for a corporate spinoff? The first and most logical answer is: subsidiaries that have proven themselves to be capable of surviving on their own. The subsidiary might be large in its own right and profitable, growing faster than its parent. Secondly, the subsidiary is often doing business in an different industry from its parent. The small subsidiary might be doing business making telephones while its parent and sibling subsidiaries all make railroads or something like that. One thing is not like the other, and it is in this situation that a spinoff would be a valid option for management.

***

As I was explaining spinoffs to people, the question that I most often got back was: why would a company possessing a profitable subsidiary ever want to remove that subsidiary from its own books? An executive running company A would want his company to show the best results that it possibly can, right? Does it make good sense to shrink the company? Wouldn't spinning off a big portion of the company make it harder for them to meet Wall Street expectations?

I have briefly touched upon the answer earlier. One, a spun off subsidiary is often doing something totally unrelated to the rest of the company. The specialties of the subsidiary's management and the parent's management are not compatible. The parent has no idea what to make of the subsidiary and vice versa. In this situation, the best thing for both companies to do is often to separate. This way, both companies can focus on what they do best without interference from one another. Now it could sell the division or take it public, but there are times when a spinoff is most ideal because it is more tax friendly to the company than the other options. So, a spinoff it is.

So, all of this is well and good for the two companies involved in the spinoff. What is the benefit to investors? Well, it is often quite profitable for the shareholders. Let me explain. All the time, analysts on Wall Street are getting together to decide how a company should do in the coming quarter. They make estimates, look at industry research, and make guesses. Wall Street investors and traders look at these expectations and use that to come to an agreement amongst one another - through bidding and selling - on the value of the company, its stock price.

Figuring out this future earnings number is very difficult. You can only use publicly available information such as SEC filings and published research. There are so many variables that you have to consider, including the macro environment, unexpected legislation and litigation, and the competition. Many people get it wrong. So the last thing that analysts want to see is a big, sprawling conglomerate with random subsidiaries doing all sorts of different things all over the world. It injects uncertainty into the equation and when you have that, then nobody knows what is going on and the company stock price just meanders. Nobody knows if the stock is undervalued, overvalued, or rightly valued! A spinoff clears up a previously obscure company by cleaving off its confusing parts. The company gets smaller and simpler to understand. Analysts can get a better grip on what is going on and as a result often bid the price upwards. So the result is that after a spinoff, *both* companies *should* see a nice increase in their stock prices at least on the day it happens.

Study	Country	Research period	Observations	Event window	Cumulative average abnormal return (%)
Schipper and Smith (1983)	US	1963–1981	93	(-1, 0)	2.84***
Hite and Owers (1983)	US	1963–1981	123	(-1, 0)	3.3***
Miles and Rosenfeld (1983)	US	1963–1980	55	(0, 1)	3.34***
Rosenfeld (1984)	US	1963–1981	35	(-1, 0)	5.56***
Copeland et al. (1987)	US	1962–1982	188	(-1, 0)	3.03***
Denning (1988)	US	1970–1982	42	(-6, 6)	2.58
Seifert and Rubin (1989)	US	1968–1983	51	(-1, 0)	3.26***
Ball et al. (1993)	US	1968–1990	39	(-1, 0)	2.55
Vijh (1994)	US	1964–1990	113	(-1, 0)	2.90***
Allen et al. (1995)	US	1962–1991	94	(-1, 0)	2.15***
Michaely and Shaw (1995)	US	1981–1988	9	(-1, 1)	3.19
Slovin et al. (1995)	US	1980–1991	37	(0, 1)	1.32**
Seward and Walsh (1996)	US	1972–1987	78	(-1, 0)	2.6***
Johnson et al. (1996)	US	1975–1988	104	(-1, 0)	3.96***
Daley et al. (1997)	US	1975–1991	85	(-1, 0)	3.4***
Desai and Jain (1999)	US	1975–1991	144	(-1, 1)	3.84***
Krishnaswami and Subramaniam (1999)	US	1978–1993	118	(-1, 1)	3.28***
Mulherin and Boone (2000)	US	1990–1999	106	(-1, 1)	4.51***
Maxwell and Rao (2003)	US	1976–1997	79	(0, 1)	3.59***
Veld and Veld-Merkoulova (2008)	US	1995–2002	91	(-1, 1)	3.07***
Kirchmaier (2003)	Western Europe	1989–1999	48	(-1, 1)	5.4***
Veld and Veld-Merkoulova (2004)	Western Europe	1987–2000	156	(-1, 1)	2.62***
Sudarsanam and Qian (2007)	Western Europe	1987–2005	157	(-1, 1)	4.82***
Murray (2000)	UK	1992–1998	25	(-1, 1)	-0.19
Schauten et al. (2001)	UK	1989–1996	23	(-1, 1)	2.13
Sin and Ariff (2006)	Malaysia	1986–2002	85	(-1, 0)	1.80*

Notes: This table presents the cumulative average abnormal stock returns around the announcement dates of spin-offs.
Significance level is not reported for this event window; ***significance at the 1% level; **significance at the 5% level; *significance at the 10% level.

The table above comes from a paper written in 2008 and published in the *International Journal of Management Reviews*, Value Creation Through Spin-offs by Chris Veld and Yulia Veld-Merkoulova. It shows a selection of spinoffs from 1983 to 2006 in the US and UK. The important thing to consider though is the column on the far right: Cumulative average abnormal return. This fancy looking word means, "How much higher the spinoff makes your stock go up on the day of the announcement!" The more stars on the right of the number, the more pronounced the effect is. Turns out the average is about 3%.[12]

A nice boost, and a notable event for investors and managers alike, if you ask me. And if that is not enough reason for you to be interested in studying spinoffs further, then how about this? In 2007, hedge fund manager Mohnish Pabrai paid $650,000 to win a charity auction lunch with Warren Buffett. From the master, he learned three things. The third of those things was to study closely the spinoffs.

***

Short Squeeze

---

[12] Here is the part where I walk back everything I just wrote about and you slap your forehead going, "God this guy is an idiot!"

Here goes … this table comes from early research and is a small sample. And the way things go in business is that one thing gets popular and everybody starts copying it, crashing the party for the worse. Other papers have disputed the findings, with more refined statistical measures finding no appreciable effect.

Does the spinoff effect still work? Hard to say, but the rest of the securities industry seems to believe it: There is a spinoff ETF that ordinary investors can invest in. Go to Google Finance and type in CSD.

A short squeeze is when a company essentially forces all the people going short its stock to reverse their trade, resulting in a huge surge in the company's stock price. How does that happen? Recall that when someone goes "short" a stock, what they are doing is that they are first borrowing a share of stock from someone else so that they can immediately go and sell the stock into the open market, taking the cash proceeds for themselves. Usually the person they are borrowing the share from is a brokerage (who in turn uses the stock owned by its brokerage customers[13]) but it can also be a hedge fund or bank. And before you ask the question, yes they are indeed selling something that they do not technically own. Well what is the catch? Well the catch is that the trade is not over yet. Just like how you close a traditional "long" trade by selling the stock you bought, you close a short trade by buying back the stock you first sold and returning to the person you borrowed it from. If it might help you comprehend the idea a little better, there is a bit of symmetry going on. In the "long" trade, you **buy first** and then <u>sell later</u>. Investor makes money if the stock price goes up. Then there is the opposite-direction short trade, which is where you **sell first** and then <u>buy later</u>[14]. The idea is that hopefully if the trade goes right then the price at which you buy back the stock is much lower than the price at which you first sold it. You make profit from the difference. It is a way then someone could make money from falling stock prices.

---

[13] Most people are not aware that the shares that they are holding in a brokerage are at many times being lended out for shorting. How about that?

[14] There are a few other differences that make it not quite simple. For example, there is a constant margin charge fee for borrowing the stock because you are technically getting something for nothing right now.

Also, if the stock pays a dividend then the short seller has to also pay the same amount of the dividend to the borrower.

So going back to this idea that a short trade is the opposite of a long trade, a short squeeze is the reverse of a stock crash. If a company that many people have gone short has announced something that spooks the short traders, then they will all pile for the door and buy back the stock to close their trade. The price leaps up a whole bunch. Sometimes there are so many shares being shorted that it takes several days to unwind them all, and the stock price keeps going up for a few days or so. This is why sometimes you would find that a company that many people think is terrible announces just a bit of tiny good news and the stock goes up some 15-20%. You would at first think that investors are perhaps overvaluing this tiny bit of good news and getting themselves into a frenzy buying those shares. How dumb they are, right? Perhaps your sentiments are a little bit true, but more likely the big leap in prices are the result of the short investors closing out their short trades and buying back the stock rather than now-excited long investors opening positions in the company.

**

So to sum up a lot of the exposition in the last two paragraphs, a short trade is the opposite version of a long trade. Now that we know about this, we can start adding some flavor to this basic skeleton to have some fun and learn some interesting things. Let us start with some of the additional differences between a long trade and a short trade.

As long as an investor does not use leverage on a long trade then nobody can make that person sell that stock. They can hold the stock for as long as they wish! Sometimes there are shares of stock owned by grandparents that are passed down through the generations. As long as they do not want to sell, then they do not sell and the trade does not close. A short trade however is different. A short investor is inherently using leverage. I say "inherently" because the short trade by its very definition is using money - in the form of shares - borrowed from someone else. And when someone uses leverage, then they are basically signing away a little piece of themselves to that second party. If things go south then that second party can basically call in the dogs and force you to unwind at the worst possible time. You want to sell at the right time, at your own choosing, not because someone said you should.

If that is the case, then might it be possible to force all the short sellers to unwind their trade? Might it happen then that all the short sellers have to say uncle and buy back those shares all at once? Might it then be that the stock price would skyrocket into the stratosphere? Yes, and it is called a corner.

In your standard flavor corner, there is a company's stock - Acme Inc - that someone - who I shall call Audrey - is buying. Audrey is buying millions upon millions of dollars worth of Acme shares. So much so that her actions are single-handedly causing the stock price to rise beyond what people would think is fundamentally sustainable (whatever vague notion that might mean). Hedge funders and speculators notice this and they start shorting the stock. They basically see an opportunity from Audrey's purchases developing. Once Audrey stops accumulating the shares then the upwards pressure on the Acme stock price will cease and then the stock price will pull back because it is not longer being supported by all of Audrey's buying. As news of this trade floats around Wall Street, more and more hedge funders enter the arena. This is the hedge fund world after all where one smart trade gets copied by dozens of funds kind of like how after

Instagram went big, everyone started making picture taking apps. But those fund managers are walking into one big huge roach motel of a trap. Audrey has been buying shares for so long that she has a huge percentage of the company. Such a huge percentage that it is getting hard to find a share of Acme to borrow because the number of shares outstanding is falling and Audrey is not selling anything she owns. Remember what I said earlier about hedge funders getting the stock that they borrow for short trades from brokerages ... who then get the stock from their customers? Well, it so happens that the brokerages - finding it hard to execute the trade properly - are now borrowing the shares from Audrey.

Now it is time for the hurting.

Audrey announces to the world, "Surprise! I have lent out a lot of shares of Acme to you short-sellers and guess what? I want them all back now. Please." All the hedge funders realize that they suddenly have to come up with the shares soon and scramble to find them ... only to realize that pretty much the game in town is Audrey herself. It is like selling lemonade in the desert to people who have been sitting for a long time in a hot sauna. She names her price - which is going to be a lot higher than "free" - and all the funders get taken to the cleaners because they have no choice but to pay that price. Audrey rides off into the sunset counting her stacks.

Probably the most famous short squeeze/corner that has happened in the past few years happened in 2008 with Porsche and Volkswagen ("VW"). Porsche and VW many years ago were founded by the same family and the companies are very closely tied to one another. For example, many of the parts that go into Porsche cars come from VW. What

Porsche executives realized is that if that source happens to dry up then Porsche would find itself in dire straits. This situation was ominously illustrated during the mid 2000's when VW found itself fighting off a foreign takeover that set off alarm bells in the minds of the Porsche family. What happens if someone buys out VW and tries to kill Porsche by cutting off its supply of auto parts? Porsche did not want to lose its independence by finding itself beholden to some other company. What the executives decided to do was to give itself a say in VW's future by buying VW stock. It slowly accumulated shares over the years. Told almost nobody how much they owned or how much they were buying. Just kept buying and buying. The hedge funders noticed this and started shorting the stock because the way they figured it, VW's stock price would fall once Porsche stopped buying and there was no reason that Porsche would want to own the entirety of VW. First, 20% of those VW shares are owned by the German government and the government is not looking to sell those shares (though this turned out to be a bad thing for the hedge funders). And secondly, Porsche's intentions seemed to be pretty clear. They want to gain control of VW so that they can guarantee their own auto parts supply chains. You only need to have 50% of VW shares to have that control. And since Porsche was so much smaller than VW - Porsche makes about $18 billion a year while VW brings in a staggering $207 billion[15] - it made absolutely no sense that this prestigious but tiny player could buy out and own the third largest automaker in the world.

[15] This data is as of 2012.

VW: http://www.cnbc.com/id/46706577

Porsche: http://www.statista.com/statistics/223258/revenue-of-porsche/

Technically they were right but thanks to the powers of derivatives they still got taken to the cleaners. We will talk a little more later about how derivatives work and their role in creating this situation but basically what happened was that one day Porsche announced that they had owned 42.6% of the shares. This is fine but then they added that they also had options - a certain type of financial derivative that lets you buy more stock without spending all the money for it outright - for another 31.5% of the company. It got worse. Porsche also announced that they were about to buy yet more shares and complete a full 75% ownership stake. Everyone freaked out and they went for the fire doors. They needed to return those shares of stock but from where can they get it? Porsche had control over some two-thirds of the shares outstanding and the German government had another 20%. The price for whatever was left out there went up exponentially from $265 to over $1,000. Supply and demand, folks.

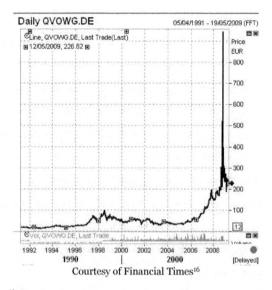

Courtesy of Financial Times[16]

Look at that spike!

Sounds cool right? Evil short selling hedge funders get their comeuppance and a smart someone makes a whole lot of money. There is a problem though. Corners like this are pretty much illegal in most countries. After all the hedge funders come back from the cleaners that they were taken to after a corner, their first stop would be to their lawyers' offices. Porsche and a number of hedge funds have been engaged in litigation for years over what was done in 2008. It could drag on for longer than it is worth.

And then there is the little issue of the company itself. You have to really want it because if the corner works then you not only have your stacks but the company too and nobody

---

is going to buy it back from you. The most famous example happened with the retailer Piggly Wiggly in the 1920s. It worked but the guy who did it eventually went broke. Porsche executed its corner well but then it turned out that the company had taken out billions of dollars in loans that it could not renew when the air went out of the market in 2008. Porsche eventually fell apart and ironically got acquired by its to-be acquisition Volkswagen. Porsche gained some serious bragging rights in the financial space but lost the very independence that it was looking for in the first place.

**

Investing In Front of Institutions

Hedge fund managers keep close tabs on what the institutional investors are looking at or are thinking about. If you can recall, these institutional investors oversee hundreds of billions of dollars and need to generate billions of dollars of returns on that money. Hedge funds are big, but nowhere as big as these institutional investors like sovereign wealth funds and pension funds. When these investors make moves, the sheer amount of money invested can move market prices in an instant.

So why do investors care about this? **If you know ahead of time that an asset class is about to get "overweighted" by the institutions, then you can make a bunch of money by owning it before they make their move.** Staying one step ahead of the institutions is a valued money-making tactic. Back in 2009-10, the Chinese and Indian central banks began to purchase tons and tons of gold (ostensibly to diversify their holdings away from US Treasury bonds). Funds who owned stakes in gold saw their returns surge. Conversely, if you know that an institution is going to DUMP a whole bunch of something into the market, you want to have been long out of that thing because if a big institution with a big stake in something sells then prices are going way down.

The concept applies to stocks in the public markets as well. **There is a lot of research that implies that the majority of a single stock's return stems from the fact that it happens to be in the right industry at the right time.** Energy companies - even those which are fundamentally terrible with bad management and economics - saw their stock prices grow by leaps and bounds during the oil crisis in 2007. This effect is partly because of the asset classifications used by the institutional investors. They identify a good industry and flood the entire group with money, sending every company's stock price through the roof.

It is hard to ignore just how important it is to know what the big institutions are doing, even if you yourself are a big multi-billion dollar hedge fund. This following blurb is from James Altucher, who keeps a great blog that you can go find on Google. He is also an entertaining Twitterer.

> The First Day of the Month. Its probably the most important trading day of the month, as inflows come in from 401(k) plans, IRAs, etc., and the mutual funds have to go out there and put this new money into stocks. Over the past 16 years, buying the close on SPY (the S&P 500 ETF) on the last day of the month and selling one day later would result in a successful trade 63% of the time with an average return of 0.37% (as opposed to 0.03% and a 50-50 success rate if you buy any random day during the period). Various conditions take place that improve this result significantly. For instance, one time I was visiting Victor's office on the first day of a month and

one of the traders showed me a system and said, "If you show this to anyone we will have to kill you." Basically the system was: If the last half of the last day of the month was negative and the first half of the first day of the month was negative, buy at 11 AM and hold for the rest of the day. This is an ATM machine the trader told me. I leave it to the reader to test this system.[17]

Likewise with Mr. Altucher I have not personally tested this so I cannot vouch for its authenticity. But the logic behind the system makes sense. Mutual fund managers flush with cash from 401Ks and IRAs see consecutive declines in the market and react by buying en masse.

***

The Central Banks

Staying abreast of the institutions has never been more vital than it is today - and it is not just about pension funds and sovereign wealth funds. It can also be about central banks. (Remember my gold example just now?) An interesting report released by the Federal Reserve Bank of New York[18] makes the case that since 1994, nearly all of what we call the "equity premium" has been generated during the immediate 24 hours before a Federal Open Market Committee (FOMC) announcement.

---

[17] Mr. Altucher writes a lot more about financial trading but lately his work has been more focused on happiness, luck, and becoming successful. It is a great, if sometimes controversial, read which I highly recommend. I would love to meet him someday.
[18] You can find the report here, though it is kind of dense.

http://libertystreeteconomics.newyorkfed.org/2012/07/the-puzzling-pre-fomc-announcement-drift.html

What did the heck did I just say? Equity premium? FOMC? What does that mean? Let me break it down for you. When academics study the stock market, they compare it to the bond market. Namely, they look at the interest rate of the US Treasury. Because they assume that the US Treasury can never default, there is essentially no risk attached to owning it[19]. It is the low hanging fruit, the safest investment in the world.

However, owning the US Treasury does not get you a lot of return. That interest rate is not very high. That is because the market says that the Treasury is risk-free. You can shovel money into it for days and never worry about it vanishing. For doing all that lazy work, you do not deserve a very high return. The stock market is much riskier. You buy a stock, even an index fund, and there is the chance that you lose money. The way the academics saw it, you have to get rewarded for taking on that extra risk. That extra reward that you get for taking the stock market over the risk-free bond is called the "equity premium".

What is shocking about this research from the NY Fed is that the traditional thinking (and the kind of stuff that a financial advisor would say) has been that the "equity premium" is built into the market. It is part of the market. Now the NY Fed's research says that it has nothing to do with any of the jibber jabber I talked about in the above chapter. Instead all that extra reward you get? Comes right from the Fed and has nothing to do with "taking on more risk". So technically, you can buy into the stock market in the 24 hours before the FOMC announcement (which happens at regularly scheduled periods 8 times a year), sell before the announcement itself, and you pretty

---

[19] Of course, with the fiscal cliff fiasco of late 2011, this might get called into question. Let's leave that alone for now.

much would have benefitted just as much as a person who held the stock market through the whole year. That is how powerful these banks and organizations have become. Not being aware of them can be disastrous.

***

Conclusion: Insider Trading

The problem with event-driven investing is that there is huge incentive in knowing what is going to happen before everyone else does. This means that you have to have that "edge". Too often, this drives managers to go over to the dark side into what is illegal: Insider trading. **What is the difference between making an informed guess that this spinoff or that spinoff is going to happen as compared to getting information from inside the company that there really is one in the works?** More importantly, is the SEC going to believe you?

Steven Cohen of SAC Capital is probably the most talented trader the hedge fund world has ever seen. He runs a titanic, very secret fund and is worth some $8 billion. Unlike many other hedge funds, his style is not all that well-known - they tend to just call him a trader and leave it at that. My personal opinion - and this is sort of backed up by some of the stories floating out there on what it is like to work at his fund - is that he is primarily an event-driven investor-trader. **Using research surfaced by his subordinate portfolio managers (who manage their own private clumps of money), he identifies events or catalysts ahead of time and puts a lot of money into it**. Cohen himself has never been accused of wrongdoing but a lot of his former portfolio managers have been. The latest case involves Mathew Martoma, who was charged November 20, 2012 for securities fraud. He had been trading nearly $1 billion worth in shares of drug companies Elan and Wyeth in advance of news about the companies' development of an Alzheimer drug. The evidence - including testimony from the doctor who had leaked the information in the first place - was pretty damning. On March 15, 2013, SAC agreed to pay regulators $616 million to resolve the lawsuits that surround the allegations of such insider trading[20]. Even for a fund that has more than $15 billion under management, that is a lot of money[21]. Worse still is the loss in reputation. In February 2013, it was reported that of the $6 billion SAC still manages for outside clients, more than a quarter of those investors wanted out of the fund. They did not want to take the headline risk and the embarrassment of being associated with an insider-trading criminal. (Martoma continues to fight his own criminal allegations in court. Prosectors have been trying to get him to turn witness on Steve Cohen but to no avail. I am somehow reminded of the Godfather Part II.)

The line between what it is right and wrong gets a lot blurrier with the existence of "expert networks" - professional companies that connect hedge funds with people who have detailed knowledge of a specific industry. Thus, there are many funds that hire these experts as consultants for the purpose of getting up to speed on an industry. But many of these experts become so because they have been working for a long time in that

---

[20] You can read more about this here on the New York Times:

http://dealbook.nytimes.com/2013/03/15/sac-settles-insider-trading-cases-for-616-million/

[21] Just in case you are wondering, that money goes directly to the US Treasury. Kind of like a donation.

industry or still have contacts there. So it occasionally happens that some hedge fund analysts ask for and get private, illegal information from the experts so that the traders can make millions of dollars from their illegally-begotten knowledge.

The hedge fund world is sink-or-swim, and there are huge incentives to make the right trade and know the most things before it happens, but funds have to be careful that all of their research is legitimately sourced, based on merit, and public. The SEC has always been good at catching on to suspicious looking trades. On February 14, 2013, Berkshire Hathaway and 3G Capital announced a $23 billion buyout of H. J. Heinz Co., the company that makes the ketchup (catsup?). The shares jumped 20% on the news. This is to be expected because the market is adjusting the price of the stock to what the price will eventually be when the company is bought out. However the day before the SEC noticed that someone had bought $90,000 worth of stock options for Heinz[22]. This is a very leveraged bet because a single stock option contract represents 100 shares of Heinz stock. This is weird because Heinz is not a trader's stock in that it makes wild moves from day to day. The stock is generally very stable because the company is not a growth company. It is very predictable. So the only reason someone would make such a leveraged bet would be because they knew that the company was about to be bought out. Insider information. The SEC went into action. It tracked the trades down to a Swiss account, had a judge freeze the account, and is working with Goldman Sachs to track down the person behind the trade. Someone is eventually going to get caught, and once

---

[22] The potential profit on the trade was $1.7 million

it happens the penalties are quite expensive. By law, the maximum penalty for insider trading is 3 times your illicit gains.

Activist Investing

Yar. Be a pirate and rock the boats, you pretties!

Events and catalysts are a tough pillar to stake your investment strategy on. Natural ones are rare and like prophetic signs of impending disasters they become convincing indicators only when viewed in the rear view mirror. So activist funds seek to make them. More often than not, they ruffle a few feathers in doing so.

It is unclear why the market would undervalue some companies' stock. It may be bad management, boredom, a fear of reduced growth, or something as simple as a lack of sex appeal. Whatever the reason may be, it soon becomes clear that if something does not happen then the stock will meander below its "true value" for years to come. **This is a terrible scenario for funds as it means that you have a large portion of your fund's capital tied up in an investment, depressing the portfolio's returns and preventing you from pursuing other ideas.**

The activist fund decides that one of the companies that it holds, LameCo, is going nowhere. The partner asks their analysts to come up with several scenarios and proposals to unlock the shareholder value hidden in the company's books. The analysts come up with a few. It could be anything. A merger, an asset sale, a dividend, or even a stock split. The end goal is to try to get people to look once more at the company.

Fund managers bring the idea to company management. Sometimes the company is receptive to their overtures but other times they are rejected. Spurned and frustrated, the partners then decides that the best way to get through to management is to purchase a large stake and then disseminate its message throughout the other shareholders. **The hope is that either they can move management through public pressure alone to undertake the suggested actions or rouse up enough votes to place a fund representative on the board where they can really work to dictate strategy.**

Publicly airing your investment thesis and actively going on a PR war with management is a gutsy strategy. **Company management has an astounding number of legal protections designed to keep their jobs intact.** Though in theory the shareholders own the company and "appoint" a board of directors to represent their interests, very little gets enough of them into line to vote over management's agenda. The cards are shuffled against you.

Still, a few managers dabble in and have succeeded with the strategy. Carl Icahn is well known for conducting these sort of activist fund overtures, buying large stakes in companies and then agitating for a seat on the board. CalPERS features the famous "Focus List" on where it singles out underperforming companies. The attention and subsequent shareholder agitation helps: Studies have found that companies on the Focus List tend to outperform the majority of the market in the years after they have been identified as a "trouble spot." But one guy who does it real well is David Einhorn of Greenlight Capital.

David Einhorn has made a name out of his shorts, which he in rare step sometimes makes public. His short bet on Lehman paid off in the long run when they filed for bankruptcy in 2008 but the gain was more than drowned out by other declines in his portfolio - as his picks are more long than short.[23] Einhorn's investment style is about buying just a few stocks (not very diversified) and picking those stocks very carefully. The man does some very impressive research. Just take a look at a recent presentation he gave on Green Mountain Coffee Roasters (GMCR).[24] It is a clinic on how to craft an investing hypothesis. He starts with the business fundamentals, looking at the overall market potential as well as the projected profit potential for the company. No rock is left unturned. On Slide 27 he looks at the Brewer penetration rate ...

---

[23] He wrote a great book that I highly recommend called "A Long Short Story." It is a fascinating look into the methodology and investing style of a successful hedge fund manager.
[24] You can go look at the presentation on Scribd:http://www.scribd.com/doc/69448474/David-Einhorn-s-presentation-on-Green-Mountain-Roasters

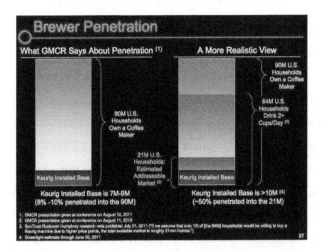

On slides 33-37 he evaluates a new Starbucks deal with GMCR that has gotten a lot of people real excited about the growth potential. He is more tepid on it ...

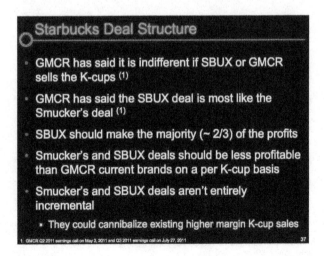

Then in slides 56-66, they go look at GMCR's patent portfolio and the coming expiration of those coffee-related patents. These are very profitable patents for GMCR and their expiration would bring in a flood of cheap copycats.

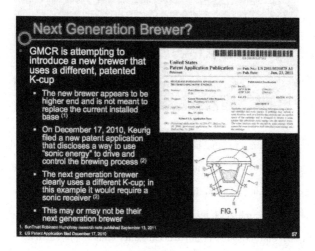

They even interviewed the truck drivers and workers in GMCR's distribution network, trying to evaluate whether or not GMCR is playing up their results.

Field Interviews – In Their Own Words

Irregularities during external inventory audits at MBlock

- Prior to the inventory audit, "We would remove product and preload trailer trucks to ship to retailers because we didn't have room on the floor. Then we'd load more product on trailer trucks to nowhere to move it off the floor."

- The warehouse was partially cleared prior to an audit, leaving a skeleton inventory of ~50%. Inventory was loaded onto trucks, which sat in the docks and was never counted. Sometimes after the audit, the product would simply be moved back into the warehouse.

- Immediately prior to an audit, 500,000 brewers were inventoried and processed as an order for QVC. The brewers were never shipped, and after the audit, the inventory was restocked.

Sources: Former GMCR / MBlock workers

97

Einhorn is a rare manager in that he is very open about his research. Few funds release their investment thesis on a stock to the general public. But thank goodness he does because it demonstrates just how thorough and exhaustive a job you *should* be doing on your investment research. Such research yields results. The stock hit its peak of $111 in September 2011 and soon after began to decline after Einhorn presented his short thesis to the public. Then in May 2012 Green Mountain announced Q2 sales of $885 million - well short of the $972 million that analysts had expected - and the stock crashed an astounding 42% that day.

Einhorn's mere presence can haunt companies like a specter. In May 2012, he made a surprise appearance at the quarterly earnings conference call of a company called Herbalife. Herbalife makes health and beauty products. The unique thing about them though is that they do not sell products to stores like Walgreens. Instead, ordinary folks buy Herbalife's products at a discount and then resell them to their friends and family. Whatever differences in price they get to keep as profit. Accounting-wise it is a tough business to trust because there can be all kinds of shenanigans that can be pulled. You will hear more about this company in a bit. While he did not at all sound combative or threatening and his questions were pretty ordinary, his mere presence was enough to make investors take the stock down over 15% the next day. There is a great interactive piece by the Wall Street Journal[25] that details second by second the effect of Einhorn's questions on the stock as it happened. When it eventually came out that Einhorn was NOT short Herbalife, the stock leapt 16%.

***

Notwithstanding the fact that you can never figure how an event will affect a stock price - that never goes away with any strategy - there is a secondary risk in rocking the boat. LPs are often not a fan of being part of a fund that makes such a splash in the business world, especially in this time of interconnectedness. **The rich people who make up the majority of your non-institutional investor base are businessmen with friends all over the industry - why would they want to be seen investing with this joker of a fund manager making these wild crazy accusations in public?** Imagine the turn a light hearted conversation at the dinner party would take. A good fund manager keeps their mouth shut while delivering their above market return. If they

[25] You can find it here and it is freely available to non-subscribers. Interactive journalism at its best.

http://online.wsj.com/article/SB10000872396390444450004578002783686418120.html

can at least do that, then everyone gets to buy their own private islands and retire young with the ocean waves licking their toes on the sandy beach.

On the other hand, these boat rocking funds are filling a vital role. Credible, fact-based journalism - the kind that uncovers Watergates and wins Pulitzers - is in universally short supply but feels especially endangered in the business space. With the weakening of the financial journalism market, major outlets are filled with puff pieces and biographies of senior executives. The business acumen, investigative tenacity, and accounting knowledge that is the cornerstone of such financial journalism are traits hedge fund managers have in spades. **Incentivized by their trades, backed by strong research, and aided by the advent of new forms of disseminating information, a few hedge fund managers have occupied a niche as muckrakers.**

And frauds do exist. In addition to Michael Burry and the well documented success of shorting subprime mortgages, I mentioned Kerrisdale Capital earlier. They made a lot of money shorting the public stock of Chinese companies. Fly by night Chinese companies with inflated accounting figures and a desire to be public in the US have realized that they can do so by listing an empty shell company on the public markets and then merging it with their own company. (This process is called a reverse merger.) The result is a public listing of their own company without having to go through the expensive and lengthy SEC approval process.

Investors with their heads full of optimism about the Chinese market (where 100% growth rates year over year are everywhere!) quickly engorged on a multitude of Chinese companies. People wrote long articles on stock picking websites, touting the stock's highly undervalued fundamental nature and the obvious explosion soon to come to their stock prices. These boosters hire Chinese translators, fly out to China to see the stores, and make all kinds of complex charts. Unfortunately they are too often lulled unawares by the fact that the company has a ticker on the NASDAQ. The numbers are there in the filings! The filings come from the SEC! The numbers *must* be right! **It all means nothing if the accounting numbers are not what they say they are.**

With one such company, Longtop Financial Technologies, the auditor Deloitte resigned and posted this awesome letter. Awesome not because it is great for the company (or the investors), but because you wouldn't think that any sane CEO would let it come to this:

> Hong Kong, China, May 23, 2011 — Longtop Financial Technologies Limited ("Longtop" or the "Company") (NYSE: LFT) announced today that the Company's registered independent accounting firm, Deloitte Touche Tohmatsu CPA Ltd. ("DTT"), has resigned as auditor of the Company by letter dated May 22, 2011. The Company also announced that Derek Palaschuk, the Company's Chief Financial Officer, tendered his resignation by letter, dated May 19, 2011, and the Board has taken his resignation under advisement.
>
> **In its letter, DTT stated that it was resigning as the result of, among other things (1) the recently identified falsity of the Company's financial records in relation to cash at bank and loan balances (and possibly in sales revenue); (2) the deliberate interference by certain members of Longtop management in DTT's audit process; and (3) the unlawful detention of DTT's audit files. DTT further stated that DTT was no longer able to rely on management's representations in relation to prior period financial reports, that continued reliance should no longer be placed on DTT's audit**

reports on the previous financial statements, and DTT declined to be associated with any of the Company's financial communications in 2010 and 2011.

Longtop's Audit Committee has retained US legal counsel and authorized the retention of forensic accountants to conduct an independent investigation into the matters raised by DTT's resignation letter. The Audit Committee has also initiated a search for a new auditor. Further, Longtop was advised by the United States Securities and Exchange Commission ("SEC") that the SEC was conducting an inquiry regarding related matters. Longtop intends to cooperate fully with the SEC's inquiry.

You can go find the link to the filing in all of its glory in the footnotes.[26]

The stock used to trade as high as $35 a share in 2011, making it a $2 billion company. It all quickly vanished. The stock no longer exists. Unfortunately for those who invested and lost money with these reverse-merger frauds (and this was an exalted group that includes Lee Ainslie's Maverick Capital and Chase Coleman's Tiger Global, two of the best funds around[27]), there is no real way to get a refund. Most frauds get sued by their

---

[26] SEC deliciousness:

http://www.sec.gov/Archives/edgar/data/1412494/000095012311052882/0000950123-11-052882-index.htm

[27] I suggest you Google them and learn a little more. They really are some of the best in the business.

Tiger Global made 71% in 2007 when everyone else was eating dirt. Since 2001 the fund has returned 21% annually. Amazing.

shareholders so that at least a little bit of their original investment comes back to them. You can't do that here. A Chinese reverse merger company is US-listed on the NASDAQ but is really based in China. American law does not apply. In Dec 14, 2011 the SEC revoked Longtop's stock registration. The company (and its management) folded up and vanished into the Chinese ether.

***

Many hedge funds are still weary of being labeled market manipulators but the fact remains: **Independent, diligent and intelligent journalism is not cheap to make and increasingly that sort of journalism is being largely abandoned by shrinking newspapers across the country.** With their implosion, investors need an investigative body of oversight beyond that which is provided by government. Hedge fund managers may not be independent, but they are intelligent and diligent. And as Meat Loaf once sang long ago, two out of three ain't bad.

Maverick just beats the market and does it without crazy risk. 6-7% better than the SP500 year in and year out.

Private Investments, Public Success

Wait, what private equity type? What does that mean? I thought PE funds were later!

It has been interesting as of late to note the interbreeding between the hedge fund and the private equity fund. Some private equity funds have opened hedge funds of their own, trying to leverage their brand names (yes, investing institutions have "brands"). And as you are about to see, **some funds make private equity type investments**. A hedge fund doing this does this not because they want to muscle in on the competition, but because a private equity type investment can be really help a fund hit those benchmarks. **As funds get larger, they start finding that it is getting harder to find opportunities that give them those returns.** They cannot buy the stocks of smaller companies because their very purchases send the prices skyrocketing and they are not satisfied with just purchasing the stocks of the large cap companies because everyone owns those already.

A private equity type investment is most often done as a <u>direct arrangement</u> between a hedge fund and a company. Let us say a hedge fund meets a telecommunications company in Malaysia. The company wants to continue its expansion by setting up a series of cell phone towers across their country but cannot find the money to do so. Our hedge fund offers to start a joint venture - the fund provides the cash and the company brings the expertise. The company does well, goes public and makes billions for both sides. Or it wobbles, struggles, and then fails, losing millions of dollars and bruising dozens of egos. Unlike buying stock in a company where the fund becomes an idle watcher, here they are right in the thick of it, perhaps even working and helping on the operations side a little bit just like a private equity firm would.

It is a lot riskier than clicking on a button in a posh Manhattan skyscraper. **A hedge fund taking on these sorts of transactions means taking on the same risks that private equity firms regularly deal with in a vehicle that is not ideally suited for the type.** In making a private arrangement between two parties, the investor forgoes three things taken for granted by holders of public stock. They are called <u>liquidity</u>, <u>counterparty</u> risk, and <u>fraud</u>.

***

The word liquidity brings up the image of water sloshing around in a cup. If there is a hole in the cup, then the water bleeds out. If you were to replace that water with something thick like porridge or jello, you would find that our cup would take a lot longer to empty itself. Financial theorists transferred this concept into their field. What financial instrument "empties itself" the fastest? What would empty itself at a "porridge like" pace? This is connected to one of the most difficult problems for investors who make their bets on private equity type investments: **You put the money into the cup. How long before you get it all back out again?**

When you own something whose value is not closely correlated to the market, it is often very difficult to sell. For example, there are hedge funds that buy works of art like

Picassos or diamonds with the idea that such one-of-a-kind pieces are the very definition of things uncorrelated with the stock market. Indeed it is like that but people need to realize that <u>once the money is spent, it will be very difficult to get back</u>. To sell a stock or a Treasury bond,[28] you set an order with the brokers. To sell art, you must call all the potential buyers, drum up a buying froth, and pay the auctioneers. That could take a lot of time, and while you are waiting you are paying money to house your work of art. The benefit though is that if things turn out right then there can be a great gain to be had. The crucial term in that phrase being "if". **The process cannot be rushed or else the price you get for it is below expectations and the investment results in a loss.** The stock in the prime brokerage is very liquid, the art in the safe downstairs is not.

A hedge fund is not normally equipped to handle items of great illiquidity. LPs often expect to be able to withdraw their assets relatively quickly. This means that the your funding is very much in peril and if things start to go anywhere south then it can quickly get pulled. **If your hedge fund holds an extremely illiquid private equity type investment, then selling it in that short time period before a proper buyer can be found and negotiated with means selling at a huge discount.** Private equity funds handle this illquidity head on - it is their specialty after all - and their LPs are often informed of and prepared for the long time horizons. A hedge fund that ventures unprepared into these waters is batting on the wrong side of the plate.

---

[28] Often considered the most liquid of all assets. This is because there is a massive pool of them out there and a huge number of buyers and sellers trading them.

A scary story about the perils of being mired in the quicksands of illiquidity. Many hedge funds made incredible returns when the subprime market crashed. One of them was a fund called Harbinger Capital Partners, run by a very smart man named Philip Falcone.[29] Harbinger soon saw a huge inflow of money from investors wanting to benefit from the next big subprime-like bet. In 2008, the fund managed about $26 billion in client funds. Imagine all the performance and management fees that the fund would be raking in with $26 billion. Falcone himself became an affirmed billionaire.

How do you follow up something like that? Harbinger's next big bet was a real doozy. Falcone poured his flagship fund into a privately-held wireless broadband company called LightSquared Networks. The company sought to build a satellite-powered 4G mobile broadband network, competing head to head with the likes of AT&T and Verizon. There are a lot of reasons to call the investment a savvy one - LightSquared has a huge amount of valuable radio spectrum to give it value - but the sheer size of the investment and the nature of LightSquared's competitors was very troubling. Then came the issues with the FCC. On February 2012, the FCC determined that the radio frequencies that LightSquared's network operated on interfered with GPS signals. That is basically a death knell and the LPs ran for the doors.

The problem is that with an investment this large and this illiquid it is not easy to turn into cash. The fund only allowed its LPs to withdraw a quarter of their account every three months. Nevertheless, the flagship fund has seen over $23 billion in redemptions since 2008 ... with a billion dollars more in redemptions still waiting to be fulfilled.

---

[29] The data for this bit comes from Bloomberg News and an article from a very informative site called FIN Alternatives.

LightSquared is - as of May 2012 – 63% of the $4 billion flagship fund. There is virtually nothing left in the fund but the LightSquared investment. So the redemptions have to come out of LightSquared and how are you going to squeeze a billion dollars out of a 4G network that has not been finished and reaches full potential in 2015 ... if it survives at all?

It is a problem that the firm has eventually tackled with a couple piecemeal solutions. The first piecemeal solution is to fulfill redemptions "in kind". This stems from the concept of "payment-in-kind" or PIK, something more often associated with high yield debt. **Basically PIK means that they are not going to give you back cash.** Instead, Harbinger gives you your redemption in illiquid LightSquared shares. This is practically worthless. **The company is not public so you cannot sell its shares into the market.** They just sit there until the IPO happens, leaving behind a swath of irritated LPs.[30]

(In August 2012, Accel Partners did a similar thing with its huge holdings of Facebook stock. Accel had invested very early on and still had a whole lot of shares when Facebook went IPO. Unfortunately the stock then did not do so well. The share price shrank from $38 to as low as $20. Accel did not want to sell those shares on the market and risk depressing the price even further so in the end it distributed 57.8 million shares worth about $1.2 billion to the LPs. Now, the Accel LPs are in a better spot than the Harbinger LPs because at least the Facebook shares can be sold on the liquid but still, it was not the ideal.)

---

[30] And there is reason to be angry. The fund has spiraled. In 2011, it lost 47% for its investors. Then through Feb 2012, it reportedly lost another 30%. Crazy.

As this method did not fly, Harbinger took steps to assuage the concerns by bringing in a third party, another institutional investor like a hedge fund, pension fund, or sovereign wealth fund. Just anyone with deep pockets and a lot more trust in Falcone than his exiting investors did. This new guy buys the illiquid LightSquared stock from Harbinger LPs who want out at some agreed-upon price. This way, the angry LPs get their money back - albeit at not-so-optimal prices - and Harbinger swaps out a bunch of his investors with just one. This is a huge hassle and a particularly rare arrangement (how easy would it be to find such an accommodating third party investor with pockets this deep?) and illustrates very well the threat of private equity style illiquidity.

(An update on Falcone in case you were interested. As of 2013, Harbinger and Falcone are still around but their fund has been battered and they have fallen hard from their high flying salad days. The SEC got into it too, investigating some shifty moves that the fund manager made in which he essentially borrowed money - money that by law does not belong to him - for his own personal purposes. After some tousling in the legal octagon, the two combatants settled by banning Falcone from raising any new money for two years. This seems like a pretty good deal for a very rich man like Falcone but with how crappy his fund has performed in the past few years, it basically ends all hope that Harbinger comes back as a legitimate hedge fund.)

Having patient capital is essential. Warren Buffett is the best investor in the world but partly because he invests on his own terms and own timeline without anyone interfering. He does not have to answer to angry LPs who can forcefully demand their money back. Instead, all of his stock investments are funded by the insurance premiums paid in by Berkshire's customers. When well run, this is essentially free money and means that Buffett can buy stocks and huge companies - which at huge size are quite illiquid - without having to worry about selling them into the market and taking that illiquidity hit. Patience is key with these types of investments!

***

If you vaguely recall the past several paragraphs, I also dropped a second phrase in conjunction with liquidity: <u>Counterparty risk</u>. People pay special attention to this type of risk when they are running private equity style investments.

The idea is this: If you go lend money to a young man, you are assuming that he eventually pays it back. But what if he does not? What if he gets hit by a truck or flies off to Venezuela with your money in tow, laughing all the way?

When you evaluate counterparty risk, you evaluate the chance that the other side of the transaction - the eponymous "counterparty" - stays solvent enough to uphold their half of the deal. You win some money on paper but you cannot collect in reality. If you make a billion dollar bet with a homeless man and win, you might be a paper billionaire but I would not go buy that yacht just yet.

In the end it goes down to the fact that finance is a zero gain situation - you made money because someone else had to pay you. Making sure that the other person can afford it is a step you should never forget. You need to consider the counterparty's credit, the nature of your deal with them, and your paths of grievance if he cannot (bounty hunters, anyone?). In a foreign country like China, where the courts are not always the ideal pathway to an agreeable compromise, you might have to modify your deal. **Better to get some real money in hand rather than staying a paper billionaire forever.**

Counterparty risk is forever present but it is more of an issue with some of the more complicated financial contraptions - especially swaps - introduced later on here.

***

An LP should never ever forget about the possibility of <u>fraud</u>. However, they should be extra careful when their hedge funds start making sidepocket investments. This is because a fund making a private equity style investment can go anywhere and do anything with its LPs' money. And when a fund is making private arrangements with third parties and throwing around fancy financial terms, the risks of having the hood pulled over your eyes ratchets up skywards.

On March 1, 2011, the SEC charged fund manager Lawrence "Larry" Goldfarb of San Francisco-based BayStar Capital Management with fraud and asked him to pay $14 million in fines. According to the SEC complaint[31], Goldfarb made an $8.4 million private investment in a company called Island Fund. The investment did very well, returning $16 million in proceeds. However, the investors never saw that money. Goldfarb rolled it into pet projects around San Francisco - a record company here and a real estate fund there - before sending all the rest of it into a private bank account. All

---

[31] The SEC Complaint is surprisingly readable and can be found here in PDF format:
www.**sec**.gov/litigation/complaints/2011/comp21870.pdf

the while, the investors got statements telling them that the Island Fund investment had been stagnating, chugging along for years at cost and no profit.

The man could be innocent. You never know with court cases. But the point here is this: With these private equity type investments the fund manager holds a lot of power, which - even if it sits unused - is threatening. The fund manager is the linchpin for the entire investment: He found the investment, signed the investment agreement, holds the contract to the investment, and pegs the value of the investment for the books. If he gets hit by a bus, that can be a huge mess because only he knows the investment as well. And if he should be someone of unsavory character then things get much worse. A manager can avoid answering suspicious questions with all kinds of excuses - secrecy, illiquidity, and more. These reasons can be perfectly legitimate, but are subject to being hijacked for fraud. It only emphasizes the importance of investors doing deep and thorough due diligence. That is why these investment advisors and the investment consultants have jobs.

***

With all the risks of investing in a private equity type investment, it is still a popular fund investment strategy, letting their potential investors know that this is going to be part of their strategy.

Such investments would be placed into something the industry calls a *sidepocket*, a separate entity kept away from the more liquid portions of the fund. **These sidepockets are evaluated separately; if an LP wants to withdraw from the**

fund they would only be able to do so from the liquid portion of the fund.
The money in the illiquid stuff waits like fine wine until it is properly aged for
harvesting. If a new LP does not want their investment to be mixed up in the sidepocket,
that wish can be accommodated.

Yet most LPs opt into the sidepockets because if done right these private investments
can be some of the most profitable in the whole fund. **A private equity type
investment made in some rapidly developing area like Indonesia is an
investment that no other fund can make.** How else can you get into this? You
cannot buy stock because either the stock markets are locked out for foreigners (like
they are in China) or the companies are not trading on the stock markets at all. It is
unleveraged private equity investing, and later on in the section I wrote addressing that
bit you will find just how profitable that can be.

A sidepocket deal arranged by a hedge fund executive in a faraway land can bring you
some wild returns. As long as they do not get too carried away, that is.

Arbitrage

What the Heck is Arbitrage?

I thought that I would bring up arbitrage because it is not only an interesting fund strategy but an interesting financial concept, period. It is a French word that means a "decision by a judge", but was first used in the context we are about to discuss here in 1704. So it is a pretty old concept. The general point of arbitrage is to create profit from two things that look the same to you, but not to the market. When the market finally realizes it, you get paid. Simple enough. But how does that work? What do I mean when I say "two things that look the same"?[32]

Let's imagine that you learned that someone can turn mercury into lead through the use of some metallic item that costs nothing and is not consumed in the process (chemists would call this a catalyst). Through the use of this chemical catalyst, which is easy and convenient to use, **lead and mercury are practically the same thing**. So if you have a situation when two things that are the same, then they should be treated as such by the market. In other words, the prices for lead and mercury should be pretty much about even. When that is not the case then there is an opportunity for arbitrage. If the prices between lead and mercury are not equal to one another - in this example let us say that one pound of lead costs $10 and one pound of mercury costs $5 - then it is

[32] Arbitrage is complicated and it is not the most intuitive thing to grasp. I highly recommend the following scientific paper that I used to help complete my thoughts:
Marshall, Ben R., Nguyen, Nhut H. and Visaltanachoti, Nuttawat, ETF Arbitrage (November 16, 2010).

Available at SSRN: http://ssrn.com/abstract=1709599

logical to say that people will start buying mercury so that they can turn it into lead. Then once they have the lead then they will sell it into the market. And once the people start selling all that lead into the market, **the price of lead will fall and the price of mercury will rise**.

An arbitrageur - that is the word we use for people who do arbitrage for a living - takes advantage of this knowledge by buying mercury long and selling lead short. Remember, when you buy something long - it is just like how most people buy stock. You buy the stock, own it, and make profit if you sell it at a higher price than what you bought it at. When you sell something short, you borrow a stock from a broker and sell it into the market immediately. Then you get your profit when you buy back the stock at a lower price and return it to the broker. By buying mercury long, she benefits from mercury's imminent price gain and by selling lead short, she benefits from the drop in lead prices. The bet is that since the chemical catalyst exists and the market seeks to be efficient, **the move is to be inevitable and the risk is zero**.

Making money off the fact that the market has yet to digest the lead-mercury news is arbitrage, where a fund profits by exploiting a market that mistakenly prices some item. **If the market knew that mercury and lead were the same, then the gap between the two items closes because two items that are the same should be priced the same.**[33] Since knowledge disseminates into the market at frightening speed, the gaps close fast. The median arbitrage opportunity lasts a total of five minutes.

---

[33] What price the market eventually settles upon would depend on the quantity of gold and silver, something I am going to ignore in these examples. Assume that there is 1 unit of each for these examples but do be aware it matters.

Only the best and fastest traders in the world - in other words, computers - can catch on and make profit from such opportunities arising in the market.

Many arbitrage ideas derive from securities that can be said to be essentially the same thing. A simple example would be the situation of many multi-national companies that have their shares traded in two or more different countries. Royal Dutch Shell, the oil company, for instance lists its shares both in London and the US. Since the shares represent the same company, they usually trade in lock step with each other. If one goes up 1% then the other goes up 1% too. But sometimes these shares are priced differently to each other. A manager looks at both, determines which one is overpriced and which one is underpriced and makes bets that the prices will eventually equalize. Here is another arbitrage situation: There are exchange traded funds ("ETFs") offered by companies like Vanguard or iShares which purport to follow the same index (usually something like the S&P 500). Sometimes the prices in these ETFs diverge from each other through the normal random process of trading. They should not since they are supposed to be all following the same thing. Two things following the same thing should not have any differences between one another. Thus, we have a mispricing and it should quickly correct itself. A fund manager can make money by taking advantage of this inevitable correction.

As you might have guessed from the fact that they only last 5 minutes, these mispricings are often very small. To take advantage of them, funds often have to borrow money - apply leverage to their position - so that they can make the return relevant for them. If you are only getting less than a thousandth of a percent from your trade then it is not worth it. Therefore you need to borrow money from someone else so that after you pay off your debt you get a much bigger profit. The problem with leverage of course is that it turns against you very quickly if your research is not up to snuff or if the markets simply turn around against you. Let us talk about what I mean ...

What if the market is correct and there really should be a price difference between the two items? For example, let us return to our lead and mercury example. To recap, you learn about this new chemical catalyst that turns lead into mercury and vice versa. Right now, lead trades at $10 and mercury at $5. You do the same thing that I mentioned before, sell lead short and buy mercury long, hoping that the gap closes for risk-less profit.

You did not, however account for a crucial factor, **the cost of the chemical catalyst itself.** Unfortunately it costs $5 to use the catalyst every time. **Now you are trapped in a trade that goes nowhere, because there is no reason for the gap to close.** Lead and mercury are the same thing so that part is right but the market is not going to "correct" itself because the $5 gap in prices exists for a reason - the $5 cost of the catalyst.

If your arbitrage participants are not as identical as you think they may be, then the pricing gap between the two items may exist for a good reason. For example, Berkshire Hathaway has two classes of shares - A and B shares. The A shares can be converted into 1,500 B shares so theoretically the ratio between their stock prices should be exactly that: 1,500 to 1. If the 1,500-to-1 price ratio breaks between the two types of shares, the movement may be warranted by the market because though you can convert A to B, you cannot convert B to A. In addition, the voting rights between the shares are different. One B share has one-ten thousandth of the voting rights of an A share. It may still be possible to make money arbitraging the two but it is not risk free because the two are not as fundamentally similar as they may at first seem.

Many funds try to ameliorate this issue by sifting for arbitrage opportunities between derivatives and their underlying securities. Derivatives get their value from the value of their underlying asset but their prices are determined by the market. A difference between the price and the value can be exploited when the derivative gets turned into the underlying. I have a friend who likes to make arbitrage trades in stock market futures shortly before the market opens, taking advantage of that instant before they are redeemed. Supposedly made money every time. I asked him to explain it to me but the nuances of his trade went over my head. I regret that I did not get him to at least put it down on a napkin or something for future review. If none of that made sense to you just now, fear not because the section on derivatives is coming up and hopefully that makes more sense.

Back to things for the arbitrageur to fret about during the night. **Outside factors and strong market emotions (the kind that come about during crisis) can wreck the laws of a rational market and ruin you in an instant.** Go back to the lead and mercury arbitrage opportunity and let's say that the chemical catalyst is indeed free. You put the trade on hoping to make some easy money, but suddenly the lead market goes bonkers because of some news report and the mercury market crashes because they just found a new mine in South Mexico. The trade goes the opposite direction of what you wanted. lead goes up, losing money on your short on lead. mercury goes down, losing money on your long on mercury. Double the gain always also means double the pain.

The Asian Financial Crisis in 1998 was the outside factor that wrecked the star hedge fund LTCM, which relied heavily on leveraged arbitrage trades for its profits. After LTCM failed, its leader John Meriwether started a new fund, JWM Partners, which crashed again in the financial crisis in 2008. The market has a talent for humbling its inhabitants.

***

Risk Arbitrage

So hopefully arbitrage makes a little more sense to you. There are two things that are priced differently, but you feel that they should be priced identically. You arrange trades such that if the two things really are the same and the price gap closes then you benefit financially. The gap closes. You make gobs of money. Rinse and repeat.

There are many variants of this concept. **One of the first arbitrage trades practiced by funds are those involving the stocks of two public companies going through a merger.** Despite what you may infer from the name, in a merger one company buys the other. It is not a "combination of equals". They announce the purchase in the news and then time needs to pass before the deal closes. This is where the arbitrage happens. Here we go. I have a fun metaphor for you!

Imagine that we have two barrels. One is full of grape juice and the other is full of wine. The grape juice costs $10 a barrel. The wine costs $20. Your boss tells you that they are going to start mixing the two to create a new diluted drink to sell to the collegiate masses for $15. You begin stirring the wine and the grape juice together.

Now let us make this a proper financial metaphor. The stock market has somehow found a way to actively trade your grape juice and wine. Only these two barrels. Previously they traded your barrel of wine at $20 and your grape juice at $10. Once the mixing is complete, they will trade your barrel of wine-juice at $15. No value has been gained or lost. There used to be one barrel of wine and grape juice each for a combined value of $30. Now there are <u>two</u> barrels of wine-juice ($15 x 2) with the total value of $30. That is the theory. What is the reality?

What is curious is that the second your boss tells you that the two barrels are going to be merged together and sold, the price of the wine barrel drops to $18 and the grape juice jumps to $11. Now that does not make sense at all. They should be both at $15. Why would there be a gap between the two prices?

The answer is that the market is still unsure that you are going to be able to successfully complete the mixing. Perhaps you do not have a lot of arm strength or the ground is slippery. During the mixing it is very possible you miss your step and spill half a barrel or more. Then you no longer have two barrels of $15. You have one and a half barrels of $15. Maybe you feel too pressured by the whole venture and just decide to tell your boss that having them separate is fine. Then you have one barrel of $20 and one barrel of $10 just like before. **The market looks at all the possibilities this**

merger can take and weighs them by the probabilities. Then they price the two barrels accordingly. That the prices are right now trading where they are ($18 and $11) means they is unsure that you can close the deal.

This is where the risk arbitrageur comes into play. He wants to make a bet that the mixing is successful. He shorts the barrel of wine and goes long on the barrel of grape juice. If you manage to pull off the mixing, then the prices converge and he just made $7. **He made $4 by going long on the grape juice (it jumps from $11 to $15) and he made $3 from going short on the wine (it fell from $18 to $15).** If anything happens and you are not able to finish the job then the prices snap back, likely to where they were but that is not always the case. The trade our arbitrageur put into place goes the opposite way and he loses money on both legs of the trade.

There are a whole lot more things that a real life situation adds to this basic skeleton and complicates the picture. I left them out because learning them is beyond the scope of this document and it starts to break my metaphor down. The fact remains though: You need to know this stuff inside out and it never goes without the chance that things can go wrong. But money was never made with you sitting on your hands. Return comes with risk - one needs to accept both.

Momentum Investing

Riding Up ... Up ... Up ...

If you are reading this book sequentially, you may have noticed this phrase mentioned in an earlier section, the one that discusses computer trading. I have only given it the briefest of overviews and the definition that I cited was, "if it is going up, it is going to go up even more". Now, if you were going to sum up momentum investing in a short blurb then that does the job pretty well. However, the definition gives short shrift to the investing style, one that has seen a lot of support and the growing number of disciples in recent years.

When you are doing momentum investing, you are betting on the notion that a stock that is outperforming the market will continue to outperform. If a stock is near its 52-week high, then that makes it all the more attractive to the momentum investor.

Instinctively this makes little sense, especially to value investors who are conditioned to like stocks whose prices are moving lower. There is a psychological effect too: People look at a stock that's at its 52 week high and feel tense. It has been theorized that the origin of this nervousness comes from the fear of heights and falling from great height. You see a stock that goes up and up and get antsy because what goes up must go down.

Interestingly enough, however, the phenomena behind momentum investing is also psychological and is rooted in behavioral economics. So why are stocks near their 52 week highs tend to continue their upwards march? (Note that people argue about these things all the time and new theories are being created as we speak. It could one of these, some of these, or all of these working in concert. Keep that in mind as you read.)

1) Anchoring Bias.

There is a great book by Nobel Prize winner Daniel Kahneman called *Thinking Fast and Slow*. It is dry and academic, but the insights it imparts is absolutely brilliant. Kahneman and co-author Amos Tversky explored the concept of anchoring bias, where people start with an implicitly suggested reference point ("the anchor"). There is a great study where they asked people to guess the percentage of African nations that are members of the UN. If people were asked "Was it more or less than 10%?" then they guessed lower values (25% on average). If the question was changed to "Was it more or less than 65%?" then they guessed higher values (45% on average).[34]

Anchoring happens in traders trading stocks too, and the anchor for momentum stocks is the 52 week high. This anchor means that traders are slow to adjust their expectations and prices for the stock. It happens eventually, just not all that quickly. If the news is good, then the stock should go even higher. But since the stock is near or at its 52 week high, traders are reluctant to send that price higher. So the stock price just inches up slowly. But eventually the news prevails and the stock marches higher. (The opposite is

---

[34] You can read this very interesting paper at http://www.hss.caltech.edu/~camerer/Ec101/JudgementUncertainty.pdf. As for the actual answer ... how would I know?!?

true as well. When bad news comes out, traders are reluctant to send the price down, so the price stays near the 52 week high.)

2) Disposition Effect.

You probably can relate to this. If you buy a stock and the price goes up, then you feel good right? It gains and gains and maybe even doubles! Wow! What a win for you, right? But then you start to get nervous. The stock is already so high and you have already made your money. You get the itch to want to lock in those gains. So you sell.

Conversely, if you buy a stock and it goes down a bit, then you grit your teeth and hold on to it, unwilling to sell and lock in the losses. Maybe you feel that the price drop was unjustified and you believe in your own research. Maybe you just don't want to take that hit. Whatever the reason is, the end effect is that you don't sell your shares into the market.

This is a human psychological effect and when this behavior is repeated over and over again amongst all the investors in the market, it tends to lift the stock price yet higher. Do you understand why? Let's do a storyboard (because you know how much I love storyboards).

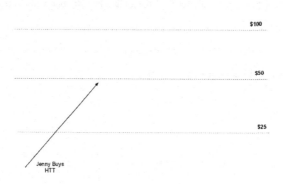

Jenny is a smart girl and she likes the stock HTT. One day, she takes all her savings and buys a few shares of HTT. The stock goes up because Jenny made a very good choice. The market recognized that HTT was a good stock and bid the price up.

On Day 30, HTT announces earnings, which beat analyst expectations and promised good things in the future. The good news means that the stock should continue upwards. In fact, the stock price should be at $100 instead of $50 (let's not argue why or whatever for now).

Jenny however has had enough. She does not know that the stock is really worth $100 in the future. Instead, she sees that the stock is near its 52 week high and gets nervous since she does not want to lose all the gains that she already has in hand. So, even though the news from HTT was very good, she sells all her shares. Perhaps her feelings are shared by other players in the market and they too sell.

The end result is that even though the good news means that the company stock should be at $100, the actual stock price does not rise to that level immediately because all the people who got in early are now nervous and have started selling shares. This sustained selling behavior represses the upward movement the shares were supposed to take and may even depress the stock price temporarily.

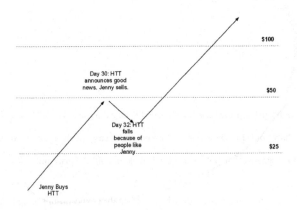

In the end, however, people can only ignore the good news for so long and the stock continues barreling upwards towards its real value of $100. Jenny is a smart girl, but her human tendencies have cost her $50 a share.

So with the disposition effect, a stock is really worth some amount of money but is unable to immediately reach that amount because of human biases. The sustained rise in stock price results from a delayed effect of a jump in the price that should have been immediately recognized by the market.

3) Bandwagon Effect

The last one is probably the most understandable. When a stock is going up, there's going to be a number of people who look at and use its recent performance to make decisions about its future performance. So, a huge number of people start buying and the effect of all those people buying and buying sends the price upwards.

Does it really work?

So there are all the reasons that we should believe in momentum investing. The real question now is: Does it really work? There are a lot of studies that look at the historical performance of stocks that can be considered to have momentum. In the past five years, almost 150 papers have been published exploring the space and 300 overall since the 1990s. All whole lot of words and a whole lot of papers. To sum up the majority of this research (and to save you from a lot of grief), the academia has been in general favorable of the momentum approach while cautioning that it is incredibly difficult for individual investors to implement.

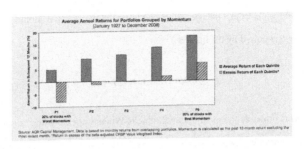

The graphic above (which hails from a hedge fund known as AQR Capital Management) looks at average annual returns for portfolios grouped by momentum. Stocks have been split into five groups with the ones on the right with the most momentum and the ones on the left with the least. If you cannot see too well, the average return of the P5 quintile, the one with the most momentum, is somewhere approaching 20% in the 12 months after the portfolio was made. This is 5% better than the market.

The biggest problem for an individual investors implementing momentum investing is that individual investors are too often drawn to stocks that have extreme momentum. The way it should be done, you look for stocks that are just starting out on their momentum runs. Individual investors however are not so good at that and end up choosing stocks that are well into or near the end of their price run ups. The result is that their picks are much more likely to crash. In other words, "bubble stocks", and unfortunately we've had too many examples of ordinary people getting burned with those.

Global Macro

The World!

In 1992, George Soros made $1 billion in a single trade by betting against the Bank of England and winning. Since 1973, he has been running the Quantum Fund, one of the most successful funds in the world. In 1997, he and his fund was blamed for forcing a number of Southeast Asian countries to "devalue" their currencies. In other words, forcing the countries to make their currencies less valuable so that it would be able to buy less dollars or yen going forward. From 1969 to 2000, the fund had a cumulative return of 400,000% or an average of 30% a year. If you had invested $100,000 in the fund at its inception in 1969 then by 2000 you would have some $500 million in your pocket.

Ray Dalio runs the biggest hedge fund in the world - Bridgewater Associates. As of January 2013 the fund manager oversees a staggering $150 billion. No fund manager manages sums of money even close to that size. More than $60 billion of that money is allocated to a single fund: Pure Alpha. Since December 1991, that fund has returned 18%, which is incredible performance. They even lay out their expectations for their fund's returns which for the most part has stayed within 1 standard deviation of that prediction.

So what do these two spectacularly successful funds have in common? They are both classified as global macro funds. What is a global macro fund and how does it make its money?

A global macro fund manager is a worldly person. His job is to look at both the actions and flows of the world economies in order to find the best investment opportunities. **They would frequently invest in whatever is necessary to take advantage of the massive global trends that they predict will play out in the near future.** For example, a global macro manager might look at the Fed's "quantitative easing" procedures as injecting huge amounts of money into the US financial system. He might think that this would lead to huge amounts of inflation. This is his investment thesis. He would then look for investments that become more valuable if that thesis plays out as he predicts. He might buy real estate farmland, non-dollar assets (which would get more valuable because the dollar is getting less valuable), or gold. Anything that can be purchased and resold for a profit is something that falls under the manager's purview. To get a sense of the sheer range of what these global macro funds would invest in, let us take a peek at Bridgewater's self-accounting of its December trades:

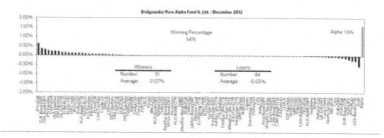

(Courtesy of Zerohedge)

Yes I know it is hard to read but it takes a lot of trades to invest $60 billion so give them a break. The breadth of investments is staggering. In December alone, Pure Alpha made trades in JPN equities, Australia Bonds, corn, gold, stock options, and even sugar. Not only that, they made substantial currency bets too: CAD vs AUD, JPY vs EUR, and EUR vs AUD. Some of these bets were successful - JPY (the Japanese yen) vs. EUR was their best performing trade - while others were not. There is literally nothing that the fund has not passed over. Bridgewater makes these bets because they think that the global world trends they believe to happen will force the investments to perform in their favor. For example, the high performing JPY trade. Bridgewater probably made these bets because they foresaw a change in political power coming and a huge wave of quantitative easing - money printing, essentially - coming from the central Bank of Japan. The government's intention would be to weaken the Japanese currency by flooding the markets with it, meaning that a single dollar (or any other foreign currency) could buy more yen than ever before. The government wants the weaker currency because it boosts the profits of Japanese companies selling goods overseas. Without doing anything, those companies suddenly are doing better. Bridgewater saw that this would happen and made an investment against the Japanese yen, which then turned a tidy profit when events turned out exactly as foreseen.

Global macro investors have a certain appeal to investors because there is something sexy about trotting the globe for investments and seeing big world-changing trends develop before anyone else sees them. Many of these managers espouse certain popular world views and philosophies, which makes for a great listen and reading. They often consider themselves as much academics as they are investors. Soros for examples likes to lecture on the concept of reflexivity - a concept that basically says that the markets like to bounce from one extreme to another. Boom to bust to boom. Dalio gives detailed talks about the global deleveraging - where entire economies struggle to recover from debt from the boom-boom expansion years. He is also famous for a detailed 100 page pamphlet he wrote called *Principles* in which he pontificates on the ideas and morals that he believes made him a successful person. It is required reading for anyone who wants to apply and work for Bridgewater.

For all their sexiness, global macro funds have had trouble delivering the returns for their investors. Global macro is a tough strategy especially in this market because of new correlations between the asset classes and the increased prominence of central bankers and policy makers. In 2012, a single comment by the Fed or the ECB could sink or swell the markets. Academic theories are great but more often than not they flail in the face of reality. Managers could not manage the choppiness nor could they predict how policy makers are going to do or react to one another. And when these funds began to see huge swings in their return - up a huge amount one month and down a huge amount the next - the investors start badgering for some stability. It makes sense - could you stand to see your 401K lose or gain thousands of dollars from month to month? What happens if you need to pull out some cash on a bad month? The academic theories that global macro managers believed in either did not play themselves out or were not given the amount of time needed to play out.

The end result is that formerly great macro funds have withered. Quantum Fund might have done very well in the past but in July 2011 the fund returned all of its outsider investor capital and reduced itself to a family office. Nowadays it only invests George Soros' personal money. In the months leading up to that event, the fund lost 6% in 2011 and had 75% of its assets in cash earning nothing. Fund managers simply had no idea on what to buy. Bridgewater, the biggest of all global macro funds, did well in 2011 but lost to the market in 2012, breaking what had been a remarkable streak. Then in the first half of 2013, the fund's philosophies had fallen short[35]. The Pure Alpha fund, the biggest "real[36]" hedge fund in the world with some $80 billion under management, was flat on

[35] You can read more about Bridgewater's underperformance here at this Reuters article:

http://online.wsj.com/article/SB10001424127887324183204578566211093933472.html

[36] Because there are so many definitions of what a "hedge fund" might be, there are some people who would call any sort of investing entity with the word "capital" at the end a hedge fund.

For instance, Braeburn Capital, the corporate entity that manages Apple's some $120 billion of excess cash, has been called a big hedge fund.

the half year mark of 2013. The All-Weather Fund, which is a fund that seeks to offer solid returns without the risk of being in the stock market, fell 6%. In contrast, the SP500 has gone up 10.5% through the same amount of time. Times change and things cycle in and out of vogue, but this is certainly not a good time to be a global macro hedge fund manager.

For what it is worth, I don't think that Braeburn is a hedge fund. A hedge fund seeks to beat the market. Braeburn was formed to manage and preserve Apple's money rather than grow it.

Moving On From Strategy to Financial Instruments

By now I have gone through a bevy of specific hedge fund investing strategies including private equity sidepocket investing, event driven investment, merger arbitrage, momentum investment, and global macro. We just cut a wide swath through the hedge fund world. I hope that you did not get yourself caught up in the jungle back there. There are thousands of hedge funds operating in the world and they all have their own strategies and ways of operating.

To make it more confusing, those funds' marketing programs do their best to try to differentiate their way to making money. Usually they try to do so by giving their investment philosophy a name. Sort of like how we give names to followers of Aristotle and Confucius, we have followers of a "global macro" strategy, "deep value" strategy, and "pair investing" strategy. Is they all that much different from one another? Is "momentum investing" really something that deserves to be called something different from just plain "investing"? Whether or not these things are just marketing creations or real examples of different species is debatable. That is a debate that I am not going to wade into with you right now. It is just too hard to say. With the markets and financial worlds being so interconnected nowadays, there is increased interbreeding between the strategies. The result is that it is getting to be harder and harder to find something that really is fundamentally heads and shoulders above everything else. There is always going to be something out there that is in vogue and has its backers, but it does not mean that it always has been or will be that way.

If you are reading this book from beginning to end in order, then the next section coming up is a two part bit on bonds and derivatives. There I want to spend some time explaining the nature of the securities that hedge funds can use and trade beyond just plain stocks.

The Safe Stuff

Right.

In this section and the next I want to explain some of the securities that hedge funds can use and trade that we cannot. If you are even half interested in the markets then you probably know a lot about stocks. You probably already go and buy a few shares of your favorite company and can make some money if its price rises. In fact it is important that people understand the stock market because it is a part of good personal finance knowledge.

However unless you are an unusually wealthy fellow then you will likely never own a junk bond, preferred security, credit default swap or interest rate swap. This is unfortunate as such instruments can be big contributors to a fund's investing success. Still, it does not mean we should just ignore it and go on with our day to day lives. If we followed such a premise then the Kardashians would never have been so popular.

That being said, you are not going to find that this is a chapter that dives in the nitty gritty mathematics of how these investments work. You do not need to know it unless you are already with a fund and are working with these things (then what are you doing reading this?) or you are studying for your CFA. I am going to start with bonds and detail the incredible segmentation of today's bond market. It will amaze you how many variations of a simple security they can create. Then I am going to work on some more

134

exotic financial instruments, including call options, futures, and the aforementioned CDS as well.

***

When you put together some very smart people and a whole lot of money, you get financial innovation. **A bond is a physical expression of a simple economic concept, that of the time value of money. You put some money down now to get more money later.** Easy enough but over the years and through many iterations of financial innovation, people have tugged at, pushed forward, and recreated the boundaries of the bond world into a Roman Empire of monolithic size inhabited by a diverse population of instruments.

You may be surprised to know that the bond markets are many times larger than the stock markets. The sizes are simply larger. This is because you need to have more money to trade in bonds (since they are issued in huge bunches of a thousand or a million dollars). The biggest mutual fund in the world is a bond mutual fund, Pimco's Total Return Fund with over $256 billion in assets under management. It is managed by Bill Gross. The amazing thing is that even despite the astounding size of his fund, Bloomberg data says that over the past five years his returns beat 98% of the competition. A stock market fund cannot have returns of that caliber with a fund that big. It only goes to show you the character of the market. Size is a huge deal for the stock market but not so much for the bond market. **The bond market can comfortably fit a quarter trillion dollar sized fish.**

There are many ways to sort the bond universe. You can do it by the issuer type or by the "quality" of the bond. **There are entire investment bodies dedicated to tracking and investing in a tiny segment of the bond market like junk bonds, distressed debt, or corporate debt.** The segments are myriad and have their own quirks and identifying characteristics. Here, I am going to start with the safest stuff - government debt - and then move along the risk line to corporate bonds and high yield.

The below graph is going to serve as your guide in navigating this long and wordy section.

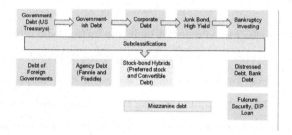

Note that I structured the graphic to give you a sense of the broad bond universes and some of the little fiefdoms inside each individual kingdom (note that mezzanine debt spans both the junk bond and hybrid debt section and I will explain that later). You can go and point to any one of these boxes and find a multi-billion dollar fund (mutual, hedge, or private equity) that deals only in that type of security. It goes to show you the sheer size of the universe. Again, if anything already makes sense to you, feel free to move on. It never helps to waste your time understanding something you already know.

***

Government and Governmentish Debt:

Governments issue bonds and that is called government debt. The debt of the United States, issued by the federal government and called Treasuries, is considered the safest debt there is (though there is the occasional spell when one cannot be so sure). Their rates are often quoted as the benchmark for other securities with similar maturities and included into financial calculations as the "riskfree rate", a guaranteed rate of return come hell or high water.

And come hell or high water, indeed. During the depths of the financial crisis in 2008, the market demand for absolute safety and liquidity spiked so high that at one point yields on certain Treasury bonds turned negative. This means the price that a person had to pay for US Treasury debt was more than he could possibly get back from holding that debt.[37] **Basically, investors wanted to pay the government for the privilege of having the government borrow from them.** Asset managers were willing to take this loss on holding US bonds - an normally insane proposition - because the prices of everything else was crashing so precipitously.

Despite what many of my friends back home think, America is not the only country in the world. Foreign governments also issue debt in their respective currencies. Such debt have their own names just as American issues are called Treasuries. German issues are

---

[37] As a reminder, a bond has a price and the price of that bond determines how much of an interest rate its issuer pays. The relationship between two is as follows: The higher priced the bond is, the lower the interest rate is. If the price goes up, the interest rate falls. If the price goes down, the interest rate rises.

called bunds. British issues are called gilts. While the pool of these foreign government bonds are nowhere as large as those belonging to the US, some have become popular and valued investments. Others not so much. **Government debt prices are cited as evaluations by the financial markets of the issuing government's strength.** Some governments are so untrusted by the market that their debt are classified as junk, with a high degree of credit risk. Goldman Sachs created and popularized an acronym for high-opportunity countries (Brazil Russia India China or BRIC) so people naturally created one for these troubled realms as well (Portugal Ireland Greece Spain ... or PIGS). Never a bad time to bring in a new acronym.

States and small cities in the US issue bonds and those are called <u>municipal debt</u>. States and cities often need money to do infrastructure projects as well as fund their government operations. People like to invest in these because of the tax considerations - the interest that they pay is not taxed by the federal government. You can make a million dollars a year in muni debt interest and have it all tax free (there are some exceptions that I will not go into - so do not take my advice at immediate face value and march right out there to try it).

There has been a great fuss made about the safety of muni debt. **Though it is rare, states and cities do declare bankruptcy, making it less likely that an investor gets their money back.** It occurs because the issuer finds that they cannot raise enough revenue in taxes or that the infrastructure project they raised the money for failed to be what it was supposed to be. So then the issuer files for bankruptcy and everyone goes to court. It happened to my home region of Orange County in 1994[38], and the incident remains on many a muni bond investor's mind. As it happens though, the majority of the investors were eventually paid back and investors should expect that. A city government has a monopoly on the land and basic livelihoods of the people living in it - it is going to take a lot to default on your financial obligations when such a money making asset is at your disposal.

If we are to continue along this sliding scale of public to private issuers, one would find here in the middle agency debt. This is what Fannie and Freddie was about. Before the government finally took them into conservatorship, they were quasi-government organizations that took mortgage loans, repackaged them, and then put them out into the market as agency debt. **People bought these bonds because Fannie and Freddie guaranteed them and the market assumed that since the organizations were quasi-governmental they had an implicit government guarantee.** It was an awkward middle way between public and private with disastrous results in 2008.

Fannie Mae, Freddie Mac and other government sponsored agencies as they are called exist for a reason. **You see, even if a person gets a very high credit score they can never borrow money at the same rates that a government or even a small company can obtain.** Without them, then our loans would have interest rates like credit cards. We would never take those loans. Without loans, nobody but the richest people would be able to buy themselves a house. Fannie and Freddie help serve this need, passing their low cost of borrowing over to ordinary folks. They sell bonds

---

[38] Wikipedia Bob Citron, the former Orange County treasurer, for additional information on the large trading loss that led to this default.

structured in a way that agglomerates many mortgage borrowers together and then give these bonds the implicit backing of the government. Financial investors reward these bonds by buying them at a low rate.

Sallie Mae is another government sponsored agency that serves the same purpose for student loans. The agency secures for students - who have no income and little collateral - a low interest rate for their loans. **These lending systems exist for students and potential home owners because the government recognized the societal benefits of having college educated people and people owning their own homes.** Just because these societal benefits cannot be placed on an income statement or balance sheet does not mean that they do not exist. That should be recognized before someone rails against the system just because it spills a lot of red ink.

***

Debt From Companies:

To be honest, hedge funds and other higher risk asset managers do not often deal in government and municipal debt exclusively as investments.[39] There are occasions where a government bond would appear in a portfolio as part of a larger strategy - some form of arbitrage or hedge perhaps - but I do not see them that often. It is more common for you to see funds holding corporate debt or commercial paper.

---

[39] Some publicly traded REITs (or Real Estate Investment Trusts) do a lot of work in agency debt. Annaly Capital Management is an example, borrowing money at low rates and investing them in agency debt paying higher interest rates. They make money off the difference and pay it out to investors as dividends.

Commercial paper are IOUs offered by companies to help them pay mundane things like bills and payroll. These are expenses that need to get paid but due to issues with timing and the way how companies receive cash it might take a while before the actual money comes in. A company with a strong reputation in the markets can issue this commercial paper at a very low yield. The company issuing them gets to conveniently pay its obligations without disrupting its operations. Investors holding cash buy this commercial paper and it gets paid back in six or so months with some nominal amount of interest.

It has become a sort of shadow market that not many people pay attention to unless it starts to sputter and fail as it did in 2008. Companies like General Electric were suddenly unable to find demand for their commercial paper and began tottering on the brink of bankruptcy despite being relatively well funded, simply because people were holding onto their cash with their hot sweaty hands. It only added to the chaos of those days. The market has recovered but it took a long time to happen. Commercial paper makes a little cameo later on when I discuss repurchase agreements but otherwise I am through with that.

Corporate debt is not a single monolithic structure. Many people like to sort them by issuers. Each of those issuers have an overall reputation and grade of their credit quality. Some issuers are very high quality and they get what is called the AAA ranking (Microsoft is one of them). It is often the case that companies of this caliber sell debt with very low yields, on par with that of some governments.

Not only are bonds segregated based on their issuers, they are also segregated by their risk profile even within the same company. That was a tough one for me to learn. How can one bond be riskier than another when they are issued by the same company. If the company goes bankrupt all the bonds get trashed right?

That betrayed a lack of understanding about bankruptcy on my own part. When a company files for bankruptcy it takes protection from all of its financial obligations, requiring everyone to pile into bankruptcy court to slug it out over who gets what. **The company's assets and liabilities are all counted up and divided, with the court people looking for a way that maximizes the value of those assets and distributes them in the fairest way possible to all parties involved.** People often times think when a company goes bankrupt it disappears from the face of the earth. That is liquidation and such a path is only one option out of many. Sometimes the company survives in a smaller state and emerges from bankruptcy, sometimes it has to liquidate. Bankruptcy is designed not as a hammer of destruction but as a pathway up out of the darkness and into the light.

Once the money is counted up it is distributed in a line. At the front of the line are essential stakeholders like suppliers, customers, the lawyers, and employees. It is kind of like a waterfall over a bunch of buckets. Each bucket is a party looking for a taste of that sweet green water called money. After one bucket fills the water spills onto the next bucket until there is no more water left. **The AAA securities are near the front of the line so it is very likely that they are going to get paid back even if the company files for bankruptcy.** At the other end of the line with the last bucket are the shareholders. As they own the company, they always get what is left. Immediately above them are owners of the junk bonds, near the bottom of the bond totem pole.

Junk bonds are securities that are not backed up with any collateral and have lowest priority. A lack of collateral means that the company is backing the bond up with nothing but its own word. So during the big asset and liability tally in bankruptcy court, you have to wait to see if there are any unclaimed assets left for you after the collateralized people (and suppliers and other non-investor counterparties) have been paid. There is a risk that there is little or nothing left. As an investor, you would likely demand a higher rate of interest for taking this risk. If you do not, you should probably do something else for a living. Grow vegetables or something.

It is this higher risk and richer return that defines high yield, bank debt, distressed debt, and junk bonds. These are securities issued by companies who are bankrupt, near bankrupt, or are already packed with a lot of debt.

Funds do a lot of things with these risky securities. Some bond investors purchase a bond at a low price, making a bet that the price surges when its market recovers. Other bond investors hope that a company is strong enough to call back its bonds, repurchasing them at a certain price, making a good return in a short amount of time. High yield is traded amongst big investors like Treasurys, agency debt, and commercial paper are. Then there is a type of bond investing that is a lot different.

***

Debt for Bankruptcies and Distressed Debt:

Bankruptcy investing is a fascinating field and the funds that do it really know what they are doing. In this section I want to concentrate on only some of their investments: DIP loans, fulcrum securities, and distressed asset investing. I am keep this focus laser tight because bankruptcy investing is complicated. This is because bankruptcy is a creation of American law. And whenever the lawyers get involved, things get complicated.

Let us first start with DIP loans. They are pronounced dip as in French dip, to rhyme with "lip". They are short term loans taken out for the bankruptcy process to go forward. Funny huh? I do not often think about how the court lawyers and bankruptcy people get paid. Yet the money has to come from somewhere. When companies file for bankruptcy, the old management steps aside and a conservator is appointed by the court. Her job is to be the one in charge of tallying the assets and liabilities then come up with a way to pay everyone in the fairest way possible.

However she first needs get paid because as your mother says, if you are good at doing something never do it for free. An auction is held amongst potential investors for something called a <u>DIP or debtor-in-possession loan</u>. Investing in DIP loans usually means good rates of return combined with a strong likelihood of getting repaid. This is because bankruptcy law dictates that loans for conservators has higher priority over existing debt, equity and other claims. Done right, they are a juicy source of return for the right type of fund.

Sometimes a fund thinks that a company is worth owning and pursues what they believe can be the "fulcrum security." What is the "fulcrum security" and why are they so unsure about its identity? So imagine the conga line of debtors waiting patiently to be paid, with the equity holders last in place. The conservator adds up all the company assets, values them, and then starts liquidating some of them to pay off the people in line. For some companies, there are enough assets so that even the equity holders at the end get something back. But there are going to be times when that is not the case and the assets fall short of all the liabilities.

In those times if the conservator believes it to be the best idea to fairly repay everyone, a bondholder can have their bonds paid back not in cash but in stock. **Usually it is enough stock such that the former bondholders are now owners of the entire company.** The converted bond is called the fulcrum and finding it depends on a good understanding of the value of the assets, the extent of the liabilities and a positive evaluation of a revived company's ability to compete in the market place. If the company is a failed bookstore - a terrible sector to be in right now - perhaps it is better to just liquidate and take what you can get. Other times you want to own the company. It might be even more of an attractive asset now that it has shed a lot of its debt. The company can be put back into the public markets for a profitable IPO.

Bond trading and distressed debt trading is a lucrative field (**distressed debt and high yield funds averaged nearly 100% returns in 2009**) with a lot of opportunities - the bankruptcy courts are almost never empty. A lot of managers have turned to taking on distressed investing with an eye towards getting their hands on certain assets. Less market trading and more private equity-ish. Here people buy bank loans on real estate or big items like planes. The bank wants to get rid of these assets so they sell the loan at a big discount. The fund takes on the loan, claims the asset, and then resells it for a profit. The reward is obvious. The risk is that of illiquidity and asset value. You have to make sure the asset is worth more than what you are paying for and you have to get comfortable with holding onto it for what may be a very long time.

Distressed debt is pretty much about assuming those risks. Lately it has been an attractive field for finding good returns. A lot of funds are raising money for investments in the asset class. Perhaps they will succeed, but the competition and the gold rush probably means that success will not be for long for many of them.

***

Hybrid Debt and Other Oddities:

Like birds in the jungle, individual bonds come in a variety of beautiful colors. Stocks bought and sold in an exchange are more often than not indistinguishable from each other. There is preferred stock and common stock. Perhaps there are a few classes of stock with little difference other than voting rights - of no use to the average investor - and a dividend. Bonds do not have to be traded on exchanges and as a result, you have a market full of possibilities, where researching the security itself can yield surprising benefits. **Issuers often look for ways to make their debt more interesting to potential buyers, because then the price they would pay for it is higher and the interest rate falls.**

Preferred stock is a hybrid security, a sort of illegitimate child of a bond and a stock. In a bankruptcy you are ahead in the line of the common equity holders so there is more likely that you are going to get paid back your investment. Also, a preferred security entitles you to regular dividend payments akin to those promised by a bond. But because of the lack of certain tax benefits (the company cannot deduct the dividend payments), one can say that the preferred stock is more equity than bond.

A convertible bond is a hybrid security that is more bond than it is equity. It exhibits the traits of a bond with its payments, and then once a certain threshold is surpassed or if a specified party desires it, the bond can be converted into common stock. **This means that the owner of the bond not only gets his money back, but if the company he lent to is a real rocket then he gets all the benefits of being an economic owner as well.** Hedge funds often structure these stakes to give themselves safety if the worst occurs and upside benefit if the best case scenario happens. Both preferred stock and convertible bonds are ideal vehicles for making private equity type investments. It gives them the best of both worlds.

Now there is a third type of hybrid security and it combines all the best of the risky worlds. Mezzanine debt is one part high yield debt and one part special stock derivatives. These stock derivatives are called warrants and until they expire they give the holder the choice to purchase stock at a predefined price. Warrants are identical to stock options, which I further detail in the next chapter, with the only difference being that warrants are issued by the company itself. **The company issuing these is often doing so because they are already heavily in debt and so has to include these**

stock options to make the debt more palatable to investors. If nobody wants to buy this mezzanine debt, then they have no choice but to sell stock, which hurts management and current shareholders. Selling stock is typically a bad sign and leaves nobody happy, so this mezzanine debt is the last line of defense before that happens.

Bond investing deserves its own book but unfortunately I was unable to do it justice. I was not kidding when I told you that the world is big. Such is scope of this document that I need to move on. Up ahead I am going to do the same thing I did here but with derivatives and repurchase agreements.

Derivatives and Other Financial Conniptions

What else are these freaks trading?

Derivatives are financial instruments that derive their fundamental value from another financial instrument. They have a fierce reputation as chips for dangerous gambles and irresponsible trades. There is no doubt that they have been used for as such. However there are more mundane uses for them too. What are they? How are these used? What is a hedge fund manager thinking when he picks up these financial instruments?

I picked out a few commonly seen derivatives for inclusion into these pages. By no means should this be considered a deep dive into every derivative out there. However there are a few that people expect you to be familiar with if you want to spend time familiarizing yourself with and understanding the asset management world. You will get your first taste of what these securities are about in the next few sections.

***

The Worrywart from Goldstown

Puts and Calls

I am a fan of parables. Let us say that in the 1800s we have ourselves a village - Goldstown - and the villagers there trade large nuggets of gold amongst themselves and the people of other villages in the lands beyond - Silversville and Coppersburg. Every couple of days a man arrives from Silversville and Coppersburg with the market prices for the nuggets of gold Goldstown is producing.

A man in Goldstown sees several gold nuggets for sale and decides to buy some. He realizes that he does not have the money to finish the purchase right now and tells the merchant that he will buy the gold nuggets later, can he have a piece of paper or a rain check for the nuggets? The merchant agrees but then suggests that the Goldstown man come back quickly as prices may rise and fall depending on the market. A worrisome development for our hero because how would he know the amount of money to bring back tomorrow?

The Goldstown man is a worrier and through his anxiety, an epiphany. He offers some money right now in exchange for the chance to buy the nuggets later, a month maybe ... and **crucially he asks that the price be set in advance right now**. The merchant balks. He has no idea what the number is going to be when the Silversville and Coppersburg messengers announce prices next month. He knows a dollar now is worth more than a dollar later. Yet the merchant has a good idea of the predicted trajectory that prices are going to take. He sees a chance to earn some money immediately by selling a rain check.

"Alright my friend," he says. "Forty dollars so that you can buy these 10 gold nuggets next month at a price of 100 dollars each."

The man agrees and pays the price. He leaves with the piece of paper in hand. A week later, shortly before the messengers come with the market quotes, the villagers get antsy and the price of gold nuggets falls to $90. **The man realizes that the $40 that he paid up front is worthless because nobody is going to spend money to buy a piece of gold for $100 when you can go to the merchant and get them for $90.** He is about to toss the paper when his cousin arrives. The cousin knows that there is still time left before the rain check expires. The tide can still turn. She offers to buy the paper at $25 and the man agrees, glad to get something for his worthless paper.

Prices from Silversville come in and gold is now worth $120! Amazing! The cousin can now go and buy the gold at $100 and resell it immediately for $20 profit. **Since the rain check paper is for 10 nuggets, then the paper is theoretically worth $200**, which is definitely a great bump up from $25. The cousin decides that enough is enough, a bird in the hand is better than two in the bush, and so meets a friend and sells the paper for $150. Despite the haircut, you got to say that the profit was quite good.

This paper, this rain check, is an option. That was the parable version. Next, we fill in the details to get the complicated financial version. Here we go.

An option is a contract between you and somebody else, called the underlying. The *You pay a certain amount of money up front to the counterparty and you now have that choice to buy that certain something at a certain price until a certain amount of time.* In the lingo, the certain amount of money is called the premium. The certain something is called the underlying. The certain price is called the strike price. And the certain amount of time is called the expiration date. Let's play a game and plug those terms into the above sentence:

You pay a premium up front to the counterparty and now you have the choice to buy an underlying at a strike price until the expiration date.

That's it. That is the bare bones of the structure. You now understand options. The rest is just filling and some deep thinking. In our Goldstown example the underlying are the ten gold nuggets. The counterparty is the merchant who first gave our worrywart citizen the rain check. The forty dollars he paid is the premium. The strike price is $100, the price on the rain check. The expiration date is one month from the creation of the rain check.

In the finance world, the underlying often is some sort of financial instrument like an individual stock. The premium is often decided via a formula that takes into account how much the underlying moves against the market as a whole as well as other factors like the expiration date and the price. **And once the expiration date passes the option becomes useless.** If you have not used it, sold it, or otherwise gotten rid of it by then it is no longer worth anything.

When a person decides to execute the contract, it is called exercising the option. Then you go and pay the counterparty for the underlying at the strike price like any other transaction. When people exercise these options, it is because it makes economic sense to do so. **If the strike price is lower than the stock price in the market, then it makes sense to exercise because now you can resell the underlying you just**

bought back to the market for a profit. If the market price is lower than the exercise price, then your option is worthless because nobody would ever use it.[40]

Puts are the opposite of calls. A put option is a contract between you and somebody else, called the counterparty, to give you the choice to **sell** something in the future. Nothing else has changed. Just that single bolded word. Repeating the above sentence once more to account for puts:

You pay a premium up front to the counterparty and now you have that choice to sell an underlying at a strike price until the expiration date.

Options and puts are contracts that can be sold to other people. Sometimes people never end up exercising an option or a put simply because it is less trouble to simply sell the option or put off to another person. So just like the underlying, derivatives have their own prices and fluctuation in prices. When an underlying's price goes up, then the option's price goes up and a put's price goes down. When an underlying's price goes down, then the put's price goes up and the option's price goes down. Theoretically of course. **In reality, option prices gain or fall based upon the demand and supply for them like virtually any other market traded item.** If a whole bunch of people bid the options up, then the option prices will rise even though the underlying's present price has gone sideways. It is all about sentiment and how people feel about the future prospects of the underlying.

---

[40] When the strike price is lower than the current price quoted by the market, then the call is "in the money." Otherwise it is "out of the money."

Options have always been on the investment marketplace for a while, but the problem with investing in them is that nobody knew what price to sell them - an issue I skirted over in the Goldstown fable. This changed when the Black-Scholes method for calculating the value of options became popular. The flood of money that came afterwards led to the standardization of the call option and option trading as we know it today.

Why would a hedge fund hassle with calls and puts? The first reason is that they always want to have a backup for when things do not go to plan. A fund may buy some stock and expect that it might go up. Yet at the same time they know they can never be too careful so they buy some puts so that if the price goes down a lot, then they can exercise that put and be back to where they were before. This is called "hedging" and is thus the reason for hedge funds being called "hedge funds."

Options are also popular for speculating on a potential breakout investment. Waiting on such an investment is an annoyance for us retail investors but for a hedge fund it can be dangerous. A stock portfolio with a large portion sitting around doing nothing dampens the performance of the stocks that are doing well and also prevents you from pursuing other good ideas a manager may have. **Options offer a way to get in on an investment and participate in the upside without having to move too much of the portfolio into it.** A hedge fund might think that a stock might go up or down but does not want to buy the actual stock. Therefore, they spend a relatively small amount to acquire the options or puts and wait it out.

In other words, **options are a form of leverage.** Note that in the case of the Goldstown rain check, the gold nugget underlying rose in percentage terms from $100 to $120 about 20%. Yet the value of the rain check linked to it exploded many times over. The standard option or put contract is usually for 100 units of the underlying. So if you buy 1 contract for Apple stock, you are actually buying a contract for 100 shares of Apple stock. So with a very small premium, you can gain potential benefit for a very large amount.

Naturally leverage works both ways. If the underlying's price edges a little bit away from the call or put option's strike price, then the fundamental value of the option will hurdle downwards many times faster.

Hedge funds can do some amazing things with options trading. There is a lot of literature out there discussing the specific trades they use. All of them require intimate knowledge of how options work and so are beyond the scope of this work. Without trying to explain the dirty details, trades can be made with multiple options - puts and calls both - so that you can make bets that a stock goes neither up or down but just meanders around at one price. Or you can buy some options and sell some options in an arbitrage strategy such that you make a little free profit without taking on any real risk. Some funds sell call options and then manipulate the underlying's price so that the option never strikes. This way they can just keep selling more options and collect the premiums indefinitely. They can play these things like a violin.

Unlike almost every other items here in this section, options are instruments that retail investors can dabble in and trade with if they have the proper approvals. I do not recommend jumping into them if you are a total beginner though so do some reading first.

***

A Thousand Barrels on Your Lawn

Futures

You may be interested to know that these were born for a purpose. It started with farmers trying to sell their products at a good price. For a long time farmers lived on the edge because the market when their product is planted is a vastly different market from when their product is ready for customers. The creation of futures helped remove that once ever-present risk. **Farmers can now lock in their prices at the beginning of the growing season and be fully aware of how much their product sells for once the wheat is tall and beautiful.** Combined with other cutting-edge innovations like organic fertilizers and those fake owls that scare away crows, it has made the farming life slightly less perilous.

As time went on, people created futures for many other things as well, expanding their use beyond the farms. **Futures were created for oil barrels, famously allowing Southwest Airlines to avoid the worst of the oil price shocks in 2006 to 2007.** Futures were created for the stock market. News reports that go out before the stock market opens note the price movement of stock market futures so to give insight on how the market is feeling that morning about … the market that morning. Kind of funny if you think about it. Many times they are right, just as many times they are wrong.

Futures are contracts to buy or sell something (again the underlying) of a certain amount in the future (called the delivery date). **Unlike options or puts, these are firm commitments - you are locked in.** You do not pay a premium up front though sometimes people will ask for you to deposit a small amount of margin for good faith. Because you pay nothing up front, the contract is thus worth nothing.

If you hold the contract by the delivery date, then you are obligated to buy and receive the item. So in theory, you could receive 100 barrels of oil on your front lawn, setting off the latest round of rumors in your neighborhood about the tenuous grip you may have on your mental health. **Fortunately, most contracts are negated long before the delivery date or settled with an exchange of cash.** And if you do end up taking on delivery well then the counterparty just sends you a receipt that points you to where the goods are rather than air-mailing the whole thing to you.

When someone buys these objects as investments, they are making speculative guesses about the future value of the underlying. Farmer Bob sells a futures contract for a hundred bushels of corn to Mr. Ling because he does not care for stomaching the risk of the price of corn crashing before he can get it out the door. Mr. Ling is a guaranteed buyer paying a price right now - and that is all Farmer Bob cares for. Mr. Ling however has studied the corn price markets and believes that the price of corn will rise as the summer season moves on. He pays some amount for a supply of corn and if he is right, then he garners a profit by reselling the corn to the markets. Since a futures contract costs nothing to establish, it can be a large profit.

Of course he can be wrong as Southwest was in the years after the oil crisis when prices receded. The airliner had continued to buy futures for their fuel, locking in for themselves prices much higher than the market rate which resulted in a huge loss for them.

Private equity funds and hedge funds making large foreign investments use currency futures to hedge the currency risk in their projects. In entering these hedges fund managers seek to remove volatility from the equation. If you have seen some of the models that these firms use to calculate the future value of their investments, they are huge Excel sheets many dozens of pages long. So much can go wrong; it is not the ideal situation to also speculate on exchange rates.

Again retail investors like you and me can invest in futures. I can see on the Internet a whole lot of sites that claim to know the secret to guaranteed money via futures investing. Ignore those get-rich-quick schemes, which often rely on heavy amounts of leverage for their "secret sauce". If such one ever existed, the hedge funds would have picked it clean long time ago. Read a good reputable book (sorry I do not have any recommendations) and do not dive head in on the first try.

***

World's Most Expensive Checking Account

Repurchase Agreements

Repurchase agreements help resolve the issue of having too much cash. Yes such an issue exists and it is one some hedge funds have to deal with. Private equity funds do not have to worry so much about it. **Private equity funds leave money with their investors until it is needed (when they do something called a capital call).** Hedge funds do not do that. If investors are giving them money and there is nothing to invest right now, then that cash is going to be burning a hole in their pockets and their LPs are going to be tapping their foot impatiently at having to pay a 2% management fee for shoving cash into what is likely the world's most expensive checking account.

Yet fund managers are nothing if they cannot conjure up some way to make money off even just cash in a checking account.

In a repurchase agreement, a fund with excess cash buys some security from another entity - sometimes a mortgage bond or a piece of commercial paper - with the agreement that they will sell that security back to them later on down the line plus a little extra for interest. **The party with excess cash gets a return for their pocket-burning dollars and the party selling the security gets some upfront cash to pay the bills, settle accounts, and whatever else to do with millions of dollars.**

This is a common transaction in the finance world and it happens often without drama. That makes it a problem when the system grinds to a halt. When the stuff hit the fan though in 2008, Lehman Brothers had been using it extensively to finance their day to day operations. At the time they had been constantly entering into repo agreements so that they can meet those financial obligations. This included employee payroll and such but also old repo agreements that were coming due and needed to be paid back. **The amounts were so high that Lehman had no choice but to wade back into the repo markets to keep bankruptcy at bay.**

The only problem was that the repo markets did not want to have anything to do with them. Lehman owned illiquid financial instruments that had theoretical value but the counterparties refused to lend cash for them. For one thing, market prices for such securities were swinging so wildly the funds had no idea if the securities they were getting would have enough value in 30 or 60 days to back up the loaned cash. **Also, if Lehman filed for bankruptcy then all of its obligations would be frozen and everyone has to go court to sort it out.** Funds trapped in repo agreements could potentially not see their cash for a very long time.

During such frightening and volatile times, people wanted absolute safety and did not want to part with their cash for even a short period of time. Lehman, trapped in a cash crunch, saw no way to pay their obligations and was forced to file for bankruptcy.

***

Your Very First Swap

Interest Rate Swaps

The feared swaps are here. A bevy of toothy financial instruments await you! In reality there is not so much to be afraid of. I find it better if you first internalize the economic end effect a swap has on the two parties involved. To me, it is more practical to know the reasons why people get these rather than intimately running over every bit of the calisthenics behind it. Thus this will be a short section.

In the bond world there are two ways people calculate interest rates on their securities. **There is a fixed rate quote, where the borrower would simply say, "I'll pay you a steady 6% for this for thirty years."** As the rate does not change all that much, there's not much else to get tripped up over.

Floating rates on the other hand base their interest rate on another interest rate number, one determined by the market. The most frequently used baseline is LIBOR, which represents the interest rate on the loans that banks make to one another. The borrower will often say, "I will pay LIBOR plus x" which means that to figure out the interest rate, he first goes online, finds the quoted LIBOR rate, and then adds the "x" to arrive at the floating rate they are to use. If LIBOR goes up one day - and LIBOR is determined by the mysterious invisible hand of the market - then the floating rate that is tied to it goes up as well. If LIBOR goes down, then the floating rate goes down. And so on.

The interest rate swap starts with two parties. One holds a security that provides a stream of fixed rate payments and the other holds a security that provides a stream of floating rate payments. The swap is a contract between the two that allows an exchange of those two streams. At certain times the swap resets, which becomes occasion for both parties to pay each other.

For all the complex mathematics and financial magic that goes underneath the hood with these derivatives, I find that they are almost always used for the same mundane purposes: Speculation, hedging, and avoiding some sort of fee or tax. Interest rate swaps are not that much of an exception. People use these as hedges against rises or crashes in interest rates, if it so happens that someone is receiving a floating rate on one security and LIBOR dips unusually low, then the person will exercise the swap and take the higher fixed rate until it makes sense again to swap. The second use for these items are, as always, speculation on where interest rates are going to go.

***

Making Money From Seagulls in the Window

Total Return Swaps

Imagine that you and I are looking out the office building window and see a flock of pigeons and seagulls flying by. To satiate our gluttonous gambling habit, we make a bet. Every pigeon that flies by is +1 point. Every seagull that flies by is -1 point. We make bets on what will be the score at the end of a set period of time. At the end, we tally it all up and you pay me $1 for every point above zero. I pay you a dollar for every point under zero.

This explains the theory behind total return swaps.[41] They are more or less bets between two parties on the total return - with dividends included - of an underlying asset. One party opens a total return swap by paying his counterparty a steady of small payments (as a financing cost). Then at the end of a period of time, the counterparty counts up the total return of the underlying asset and pays if there is a positive return on the asset or gets paid if there was a negative return. **Basically the first party managed to receive the economic return of owning the asset without having to acquire and hold the asset at all.**

The benefits of the total return swap are obvious. It lets hedge funds participate in the gains of a stock or a bond without ever needing to buy it[42]. You can purchase a total return swap on North Korean debt if you feel like it. The counterparty only needs to check the price at the end of the period of time and figure out if the bond had appreciated or depreciated in value since the time the contract was opened. There was no need for anybody to own the actual asset; it is essentially horse-betting ... with leverage.

It can get even weirder if we wished. **We could make Total Return Swaps based on the GDP of Brazil, the exchange rate between the North Korean won and the dollar, and much more.** Even the gulls and pigeons bet that we started with at the beginning of the chapter ... yes, that is theoretically possible too.

---

[41] These can also be called Contracts for Differences as those were created to avoid certain Stamp Taxes in London but serve the same purpose.
[42] Much more importantly, the funds do not even need to tell anyone that they had bought it. This is helpful for eluding pesky disclosure regulations, which might give away a fund's hand to its competitors.

It is hard to track these. There is no established exchange for them and so they trade over the counter, meaning they must be arranged between yourself and your counterparty. The result is that we have no real idea how popular they are. I have seen CFDs in more than a few hedge fund portfolios but due to the margin requirements they take up only a small portion of the overall investments. They sound like such a great deal. **Why are they not more popular? The reason for this comes not so much from the hedge fund side but instead the side they are making the bet with: The counterparty.** The counterparty - the other side - wants to always be able to hedge against the possibility of paying out a large amount, so they hedge by taking the opposite position for a net impact of zero. If you are the counterparty and a fund asked you to write a total return swap based on seagulls flying across a window, how can you hedge against that? You might end up paying a trillion dollars and go bankrupt as a result.

So your broker is not exactly going to jump at the opportunity to write your seagull total return swap but they might end up at least thinking about it. They might send some smart Ivy League analyst off to somehow try to calculate the probable profit they could get. After all, the fees associated with writing the swap would probably be quite juicy. **In fact, brokers love virtually all of these derivatives because a fund that just trades stocks and bonds offers very little in commissions.** Brokering derivatives such as swaps and options are a huge profit generator and is partly the reason so many new ones are being developed. A new financial instrument means a new something you can charge someone for.

***

Bankrupting Your Local Insurance Company

Credit Default Swaps

Same as how you can buy insurance on your house for protection from flood, fires, earthquakes and the defecation of unusually large dogs, you can purchase "insurance" for protection from bond default. These swaps are called Credit Default Swaps, and they are agreements between two parties. Here, Jenny - the "protection buyer" - pays April - the "protection seller" - a quarterly stream of payments so that if the feared event happens and the bond defaults Jenny receives a lump sum payment to cover her loss. If the bond does not default by the time the contract is over then April gets to keep all the payments and book what is essentially free profit.

It sounds a lot like insurance, but I would not make that statement to a financier. They would probably lecture you for making the comparison. Indeed, there are real differences between the two, especially regarding how the business works on the counterparty side. Probably the most important difference you should know is that a CDS pays its holders a lump sum calculated by a market formula. An insurance contract pays only the loss actually suffered and only to the people to whom the loss occurred. **I feel, however, that the insurance metaphor is the fastest way someone can get up to speed on what these things are. Just keep in mind that it is not a one to one relation.**

As usual, something a person can use for hedging and protection functions also becomes a great way to bet money on something happening. **When John Paulson famously went short on subprime mortgages in 2007, he did so not by selling short mortgage bonds but by purchasing their CDS insurance.** It adds significant leverage and for him it was an easy way to participate on the downward movement on those securities while forgoing a lot of the risk. If he had sold the securities short he would have had to put a lot more money on the line. And what if the subprime bonds gained in price? Based on the laws of short selling he technically has to be able to come up with the money for those securities. No, short selling is actually a terrible way to go short. Buying a simple CDS contract does the job just as well with leverage and less risk. (Theoretically at least)

You value the credit default swap as a "spread", the amount you need to pay the protection seller to keep the contract valid. Looking at CDS spreads has become a great way to evaluate market sentiment on a certain country or bond. Today, these are quoted on the bonds of countries with wobbly finances such as Greece and Ireland: The more the market feels that the bonds the CDS is protecting is going to default, the more insurance they buy on the bonds, causing the spread to widen. Does it really mean that the country is going to default on its obligations? Not on its own, no. After all a CDS spread is just telling you what the market is betting on. In the end, a country most often defaults when it decides on its own that it is not going to pay back its debts.

As it turns out, buying CDS's on bad subprime bonds may not be the home run you think it can be if it turns out the other side cannot pay. Counterparty risk became a huge focal point during the financial crisis. Insurance companies like AIG underwrote many of these CDS because their models told them that default was very unlikely. As a result, they took the premiums and essentially made free profit off them. Things were good until it came time for the insurance to actually matter. Having never come across an incident like 2008, when so many bonds were about to default, they found that all the money that they had been paid for writing protection for their bonds was not enough to balance out the outflows of cash that they would soon have to pay. **Realizing that if the insurance failed the entire market would wobble and collapse in a steaming pile of mess, the government stepped in and made several capital infusions that eventually kept the system going.**

A CDS contract can be made between any two parties with no regards to any centralized authority. This is different from stocks, where the majority of trading is centralized through exchanges like NYSE, and **the result is that firms can theoretically write contracts of protection many times over on the same bond.** This turns it into a powerful instrument of speculation and sort of bastardizes its original purpose.

Such behavior riles people up, as people often feel that these items should be held just for hedging, but that probably can never be a case. As long as derivatives exist, they can be used for making bets. And as long as they are going to be used for making bets, then people are going to lose money on them. The most visible example is the $6+ billion JPMorgan & Chase lost in the 2012 London Whale incident. JPMorgan's Chief

Investment Office had apparently bought them to "hedge" risk. Unfortunately, they were hedges only in name. In the end the hedge became the bet and the bet became a loss.

***

I read a lot about derivatives' destructive abilities as well as their powers of deception. Swaps and other derivatives played a big role in the collapse of several economies like Greece or Ireland because they allow banks to hide huge amounts debt off their balance sheet. This way, banks can appear to have reached certain bank reserve thresholds and avoid further scrutiny. In reality though, these banks have not become any more protected. It is simply lipstick on a pig. During the financial crisis, the roles that swaps played in the whole drama sent some politicians through the roof. The fact that most of AIG's swaps went to big investment banks and that these bankers had started creating derivatives of derivatives of derivatives did not help to smooth things over as well.

Most of these moral and economic issues are beyond the scope of this document. I have never seen a hedge fund use a derivative for something like hiding debt on a balance sheet. Managers use them as hedging or speculation. When you hedge, the net effect is zero so nothing happens there. When you speculate, you can lose it all but today's economy can absorb a big hedge fund's implosion.[43]

---

[43] LTCM's near collapse was probably the only time a fund threatened the economy. Their troubles stemmed more from a close association with the banks as well as an excessive use of leverage. A thousand times leverage it seems like. After the disaster of LTCM, banks beefed up their systems and risk measures.

In 2006, Amaranth Advisors collapsed after some bad trades in natural gas futures. Its liquidation happened with nary a whiff of panic and the economy chugged on as before. At its peak the fund managed $9 billion. LTCM opened at only $1 billion. People do learn their lessons ... sometimes.

Who knows what is going to happen with the regulation of these securities. I certainly do not. The government wants to do them but the banks find them to be great generators of profit. The resulting lobbying war has been epic. Keep an eye on the news as this story continues to develop from day to day.

So that is the end of my bit on bonds and derivatives. It was a long difficult chapter because you have to make some hard decisions on what to include and what to omit to keep the whole thing coherent and easy to follow. Like I said before, please do not use this to study for your CFA. If you are reading this from beginning to end, then up ahead is private equity. I promise that things get a lot easier to understand.

Private Equity

My favorite subject.

Though I have had a lot of exposure to hedge funds, my deepest passion lies with private equity. I started in private equity and worked in private equity all through college. If one could say that I know anything then I know private equity. It is one of my favorite things to talk about. My friends wish I had normal hobbies like Starcraft or something.

You can find a lot in common between the hedge fund and the private equity fund: There is a general partner and many limited partners. The investors are often institutional investors from the US and abroad. There is an incentive fee and a management fee. The fees are often quite garish. Everybody gets garishly rich retire to private islands in the Bahamas. But if they were exactly the same then this book would be a lot shorter and you would be off reading Twilight right now. Unfortunately for Bella, they are not.

The term private equity refers to a type of transaction. **It is about finding things to invest in that are not publicly traded like family-owned companies, buyouts, sweetheart deals with public companies, and joint ventures in foreign lands.** Hedge funds can also make private equity type deals in their little sidepockets but the majority of the universe is populated by the private equity funds that make these things their exclusive focus.

Private equity's selling point is that because their investments are not publicly traded, it is possible to invest for the long term outside of the craziness of Wall Street. Investments made by private equity companies are "marked" or valued by either themselves or a third party company brought in to evaluate the investment. The firm calculates all the paper gains that they have brought in and tell their investors that it was a good year. You can understand that there may be some conflicts of interest associated with such a method. Yet one can also see that there really are times when the investors out there in the markets are overly optimistic or pessimistic about the economy and make misjudgments in the valuation of a stock or a bond. **When a company is private, it can be "marked" closer to what people will call its true value outside of whatever turmoil is going on in the public markets.**

The challenge of running a private equity investment is that once you take on the investment you are running the company. Most of these companies are troubled and bringing them back can be a real bear of a task. Though you can select some smart managers and consultants, in the end the buck stops with the private equity group to pull a dollar value out of the company. Their success is in their hands.

I want to start with the leveraged buyout - the device through which private equity became *private equity*.

A Long Winded Example of an LBO

Just be glad it does not take as long as the real thing.

When people think of private equity, they think of leveraged buyouts. Big bruising fights between PE firms and public companies, a match of wits between billionaire titans. But what is a leveraged buyout? How does it work?

If it helps, you can think of a <u>leveraged buyout</u> as a **very fancy mortgage**. The difference is that **instead of a house you buy a company and you do not intend to hold the company for 30 years or longer**. You buy out all of that company's shares with the help of money borrowed from the market. After some years, you put it back into the market once the windows are washed, the cobwebs cleaned out and new paint job is applied.

It begins with a scene straight out of the *Godfather*. The company is approached by a private equity firm who presents them with an offer they cannot refuse: the opportunity to no longer have to worry about the slings and arrows of trading on the public market. If the company says yes then the private equity firm makes an offer to the public - a tender offer - to pay every shareholder a princely sum for their shares.

It is often a lot of cash, but the PE firm is not going to shell out of their pockets for the whole thing. **Continuing the time honored tradition of OPM (Other People's**

Money), the firm is going to mortgage to the max and beyond that to hit that final purchase price. They issue collateralized bonds, they issue junk bonds, they issue pretty much whatever it takes. Once the buyout closes, the company disappears out of the public spotlight into the PE group's portfolio. Operational or strategic changes to the company are made to improve its performance. After many years the PE firm sells the company off or goes IPO and puts it back on the market.

Sometimes the company says no. One of the most famous books in business tells a story that went down that route. It is called *Barbarians at the Gate* and is an epochal chronicle of the infamous battle between private equity firm Kohlberg Kravis Roberts (KKR) and the management of conglomerate RJR Nabisco. **Adjusted for inflation it is still the largest private equity buyout ever completed.** KKR eventually won a fierce bidding war between itself and a competing investor group, but kind of like at the end of a heated eBay auction the high price gave the winning firm a case of indigestion. It took KKR years to finally get the investment off their books and the investment did not turn out to be the winner people imagined it to be. For all the history that this vicious fight made, it is unlikely to happen again to such an extent. Today virtually every leveraged buyout is a friendly one.

Wall Street loves an LBO. Everybody gets paid. A billion dollars went out the door in fees during the RJR-KKR auction. **Investment banks get to make and sell securities, lawyers get to charge time to write up complex agreements, and consultants get paid for opinions on the company's value.** For us, it is a unique opportunity to see a lot of the moving parts in Wall Street. Let's walk down a very comprehensive example.

***

One day, established private equity firm HTT approaches a large company, OpCo Group, identifying them as a potential buyout candidate. HTT's pitch is made up of these points: 1) A private equity run company does not need to file public disclosures every quarter and so can concentrate on long term goals rather than meeting the short term mark set by Wall Street. 2) If the stock has been in the dumps for a long time, an LBO gives them the chance to give the shareholders a robust return for their loyalty. 3) HTT brings in a stable of top talent and connections that any company would lust for and as any company knows, networking is everything. OpCorp loves this and decides that they will go forward with the buyout. They negotiate the buyout price and announce it to everyone with a press release.

I have included a simple graphic to guide you through the first part of this story. It describes both halves of the buyout. First, **what do they need to pay for** and second, **where they are getting the money for it**:

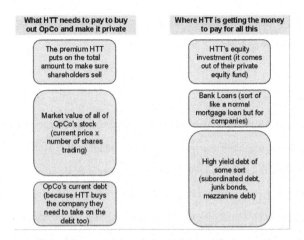

What HTT needs to pay to buy out OpCo and make it private	Where HTT is getting the money to pay for all this
The premium HTT puts on the total amount to make sure shareholders sell	HTT's equity investment (it comes out of their private equity fund)
Market value of all of OpCo's stock (current price x number of shares trading)	Bank Loans (sort of like a normal mortgage loan but for companies)
OpCo's current debt (because HTT buys the company they need to take on the debt too)	High yield debt of some sort (subordinated debt, junk bonds, mezzanine debt)

Note the left column. To own a company you need to buy up **all of its outstanding shares**, meaning all of the shares currently trading in the market right now. However, the people holding those shares right now are not going to sell those shares unless they can make a good profit doing so. As a result, HTT needs to offer a price that is at a **premium to the current stock price**. Usually a premium of 30% is what you most often find in buyouts though some firms go all the way to 50% and some go as low as 20%. (There are often times when an LBO price would be announced and some big shareholder grumbles that it is not enough to get them to sell. If it gets really bad, they might all go to court or arbitration to try and settle it.) In the last blue box, **OpCo's current debt**. If OpCo already owes debt to some people when HTT launches its LBO, then the private equity firm is going to also have to take that debt on as well. That total amount gets rolled into the cost of buying out the company. It is a substantial cost to the

LBO that many people forget and it means that HTT is going to raise a whole lot more money than just the company's equity value.

So the big question: Where is all that money coming from? **Over the years an increasingly complicated financial structure has sprouted and grown to meet those purchase prices.** In the beginning, there was no way to get that kind of money. No bank would want to lend someone billions of dollars to load up a company with debt. They would have to keep the loans on their books and it would ruin them if the company defaults. The bond markets agreed with this sentiment. A company with a lot of debt is risky and the market then was not comfortable with that amount of risk. It would be an understatement to say that that attitude has changed.

The first wave of debt comes from the banks. **They are bank loans very similar to that we would get for our home mortgages.** Like the mortgages it is backed by certain assets held by the company like a dump truck or a building. Because these assets have value a bank can always seize that asset and sell it to make back some of their loan amount. Also like a mortgage they have certain <u>covenants</u> that OpCo has to abide by. A covenant is a requirement imposed by the bank, so that the bank knows that the company is staying healthy enough to pay off the loan. For example, one common covenant I see is that the portfolio company has to keep its EBITDA to Interest coverage ratio above some number, let's say 2.0x.[44] If it fails to do that, then the covenant is breached and the entire amount of the loan becomes due immediately.

---

[44] EBITDA is an accounting measure used by finance types as a proxy for the amount of cash the company makes every year. That basically means that OpCo has to maintain an inflow of cash twice the size of its interest payments.

It is more than likely that bank loans alone are not enough. **The problem for HTT is that any remaining gap between what they can raise and the purchase price has to come out of their own pocket. This basically hurts their final return.** As a result they need some alternative way to raise debt beyond just banks. The answer is high yield debt. This includes junk bonds and mezzanine debt, two securities I discussed in my last section. Feel free to flip to them now, but basically high yield debt is just debt that is backed only by the company's own word. As you might expect, they are very risky. In order to accept that amount of risk, the bond market is going to demand a handsome reward (sometimes they want rates as high as 16% or more).

HTT is going to try to issue as much high yield debt[45] as it can. It is going to be a tough balance, because too much debt is ruinous. Every additional million dollars of high yield that OpCo takes on, the bond market judges the company that a little riskier to lend to. So if OpCo wants yet another million in high yield, the market is going to charge an interest rate that goes even higher. Eventually it gets to the point that the necessary interest rate is so high that the company will bankrupt itself paying that debt (**usually the highest interest rate they can accept is about 20%, which amazingly enough is still lower than your credit card rate**). Then for one last hurrah, HTT brings out the mezzanine debt, high yield debt that has a number of stock options attached to it. It is hoped that adding that stock option "gimmick" can woo the debt buyers into charging a lower interest rate.

---

[45] You can read a lot more about high yield debt and mezzanine debt, which I am about to mention in a few lines, in the section on corporate bonds.

The rest of the money has to come from the fund's own pocket. That is the fund's investment and like with all home mortgages, it is the first to shrink if the investment does not turn out as well as first hoped. Depending on how much debt that the private equity fund was able to finagle for the deal, the equity portion might be about 20-30% of the entire deal. Remember, the more equity that they have to put in, the smaller the final return is going to be.

So who buys the debt issued in a LBO? A whole lot of people, including institutional investors. Northern and HTT fly across the country, drumming up investor interest from governments, pension funds, or hedge funds looking to fill out the riskier portions of their portfolio. **How well a debt offering does depends on the company and the PE firm backing it, and rosters of well regarded names tend to do well.** All those organizations are potential customers for the bonds and do tend to buy in. A few private equity firms have hedge fund subsidiaries of their own and those sometimes invest in the bonds too.[46] Some widely traded junk bonds are packaged into ETFs - the hottest thing in the retail investor world today - which means that ordinary folks like you and me can buy a piece of these for our own portfolios.

If that last one sounds unsavory to you, perhaps I can convince you to reconsider. **In a time when the yield on a Treasury bond is about 2%, a high yield ETF can bring in 8-9% a year.** The ETF packaging means you are diversified so a single default would not be ruinous. Junk bonds as an asset class show similar ten year returns as stocks do without as much price fluctuation. And though the bonds are not backed by

---

[46] I am going to talk a lot more about these private equity owned hedge funds in the section called … Private Equity Funds Owning Hedge Funds. Not a creative title I know.

hard assets, investors do have a high claim in bankruptcy court because a junk bond is still a bond. So what I am saying is that it is not like these are being shoved down people's throats. They can be appealing investments. Layman investors frustrated with the low amount of interest they are getting from stashing their cash in checking accounts should look into junk bond ETFs.

The market for junk bonds does a lot better when interest rates are low. There is a lot of money sloshing around in the economy and people are often willing to lend it to PE firms for their LBOs. This is why the largest buyouts tend to happen in cycles.

So that is where the money is coming from and what it is paying for. In this section I gave you the first taste of what an LBO is going to be like. Broadly you can say that it is a mortgage, buying a large company. You are buying out all of its shares, replacing its current debt, and paying the current stockholders a high enough premium to make sure they are okay with selling. You pay for this with a lot of debt, issuing all kinds of bonds from the safe to the not so safe. In the next section I am going to tell you why HTT is spending that money in the first place. What is so great about OpCo? What are they looking for?

So Why This One?

What does a company have to do or have to be to make it a good PE investment?

Back to HTT and OpCo: *HTT has secured a massive amount of money and on a certain day the transaction closes. HTT pays every shareholder cash for their stock and OpCo removes itself from the public markets, disappearing into the private shareholder black hole. They no longer have to report to loud and noisy shareholders. They no longer have to pay for costly regulations so that they can be fit for the loud and noisy shareholders. They no longer have to worry about the stock price dipping low or being undervalued by the loud and noisy shareholders. Life, at first glance, is dandy.*

You have probably asked the question by now: What does OpCo actually do?

It is not enough to just say that the company is a good company. It is useless babble because we have no idea what the term means. **In an LBO, you buy every share of a company. Why buy all of it if you are not convinced that you are making a good investment? If that is case then you should not buy a single share at all.** Instead, HTT's partners are looking for something that meets certain criteria, dictated to them by the nature of the buyout itself. A huge amount of buyout debt means a big interest bill that has to be paid on time every time. OpCo's business nature must address that.

***

Ideally, OpCo generates cash. Lots of it. Note I did not say "profits". I said a cash generating company. Believe it or not, cash and profit are different things, and their differences relate to accounting rules.

Companies do not calculate their profits the same way that we humans do. I run my life on cash flow. Every two weeks I get a paycheck and I deposit the cash into my bank account. Every month I get a bill from AT&T charging me for wireless service. I pay it with cash. Hopefully at the end of the month I have more cash than I had at the beginning of the month.

A business using specific accounting rules sees this situation in a whole new light. Even though I get a $200 paycheck every two weeks, technically I am earning that paycheck every day of those two weeks I work right? So after a hard day's work, I can go home and write down into my notes that I earned $20 ($200 divided by the 10 days I work). I have not really received the cash yet ... but **I earned it** so I am free to record it as already mine. At the same time I need to apply this logic to my expenses too. I only shell out once a month for my $30 wireless bill but you can also say that I spent $1 every day for the whole month ($30 divided by 30 days in a month) because I have been using my beautiful iPhone that entire time. As long as you are using the product you are paying for it. The accounting should reflect that. So at the end of the workday, not only do I record the $10 in paycheck I earned but also the $1 in wireless costs I spent. This is how large businesses do their financials and it is called "accrual accounting".

For the most part it really is just a matter of timing. A company that makes a lot of profit tends to also make a lot of cash. The biggest difference between cash and accrual refers to something called "depreciation". **Depreciation is a charge that the accountants apply every year to calculate the wear and tear on an asset.** You buy a car and drive it for several years. It loses value in the open market every year. The tires get old, the body gets rusty and the seats get weird stains on them. Depreciation is a phantom cost created by the accountants to record the money you will have to spend replacing the tires, repainting the body, and changing the seats. If in reality you decided that you can get away with it and skipped doing those maintenance things, then you get to keep the cash you would have spent on it. At the end of the month when you look at your finances, you would find that the <u>month-end cash flow is much higher than the accrual profit</u>. That is mostly because of the depreciation.

If a company could be compared to that car above, then a cash generating company would run for an extended period of time, gather up dents and scratches, and still work like a charm. Year in and year out it is going to churn out money for you without you having to spend through the nose to keep it running.

Cash generating companies have business models that make money by selling something that is easy for them to make but people are willing to pay high prices for. The products were created and marketed long ago, and the company is in a strong established position.[47] The type of industry tends to be the best indicator of whether or not a company is a good cash generator. Some industries make it easier to churn out cash while some do not. For example, food retailers are tough buyout candidates because intense competition forces them to spend so much on their business.

---

[47] Business-speak translation would be: Mature companies with competitive moats featuring high cash flows and low CapEx.

OpCo as a food retailer must continually lower their prices and invest money on upgrading and cleaning stores so that their customers will not defect to WalMart, Target or Safeway. Their depreciation rates are very high, and it is depreciation that really does need to be spent to keep the car running. That is money that could have been used for paying down debt or rewarding shareholders.

For this example, I chose for OpCo to sell <u>database software to businesses</u>. This is an ideal cash generating business. Software can cost a lot to develop but once completed it takes only pennies to distribute. Once the development costs are made back every sale after that point is pure profit. However, a software company can squeeze a lot more money than that out of its software. A business customer who buys OpCo's software then needs OpCo's technicians to come out to install it and get it working with their old systems. OpCo charges them for that. Then best of all, OpCo can sell its customers a warranty to service it when things go wrong. If the software does its job well, OpCo gets paid every month for making sure nothing happens. Depreciation costs, if they are taken in the first place, are less mandatory. You do not have to spend huge sums year after year to keep the machine running. The truck takes hits but keeps on trucking.

This business model combined with the predictable nature of the enterprise market means that HTT can figure out exactly how much debt the company can handle. Once they have figured that out then they can calculate the highest price they want to pay for the company.

***

In addition to the business model, **HTT is going to look at the worth of the assets that the potential buyout target has on their balance sheet**. Here is why. On a balance sheet, there are assets, liabilities and equity. Assets must equal the sum of the liabilities and equity. That means for every asset that the company owns, like a dump truck or a building, it must assign a number for tallying into the balance sheet. How do they get this number? **For some assets like stocks, bonds, and cash on the balance sheet, they most often use the market value.** The balance sheet tells you exactly how much you can expect to get back from liquidating those assets. **For other assets though, like that dump truck or building, the accountants use a modified version of cost** (how it is modified is not particularly important here). Cost is how much the company paid for it.

But here is the thing - the cost number is not the same as the market value number. Perhaps the asset got much more valuable in the years after the company bought it. Or maybe the company got a reduced price on the asset. Yet you would not be able to learn this from looking at the balance sheet because the accounting rules does not allow the company to record the "market value" number for the asset. Only the "cost" number.

Here is a real world example: What is a wireless telecom company's most valuable asset? For Sprint Wireless, it is not its towers, its retail stores, or even its fine customer service but instead the spectrum over which customers' calls, texts, and data run. Without those bands of spectrum - licensed to them by the government - the company is worthless. If you were to dive into Sprint's books and look for those licenses, you would find that they are held at cost, which in Sprint's latest annual report totals about $20 billion. If Sprint were to figure that it had enough spectrum and decides to sell it to AT&T, AT&T would pay many times that amount. After all, AT&T paid $50 billion to buy T-Mobile with the express purpose of acquiring its licenses.

So the balance sheet can be a treasure map hiding seemingly ordinary assets that are actually very valuable. **Using their superior networking abilities and fast moving deal teams, a private equity group can find very high prices at which to sell these assets.** When Blackstone bought Equity Office Properties - a real estate company - in 2007 for a total of $39 billion, it arranged and closed multiple real estate deals as soon as the buyout closed and right off the bat start paying off that LBO debt.

I do want to include a hidden asset in the OpCo example. However it is not going to be radio spectrum from the FCC but instead an small and obscure subsidiary business: a Chinese car parts retailer. How such a random company came to be a part of the OpCo family who knows or cares; the only important thing is that it is a segment ignored and hidden on the balance sheet. OpCo's old management did not care much for this tiny company. They do not know how to run it. HTT on the other hand recognizes a growth opportunity. There is a huge potential market for the business. Millions of people are getting richer in China and as they get wealthier they get cars. Those cars break down. When such a thing happens you can sell car parts to fix those broken cars. HTT does not take long to determine that this small subsidiary is an asset worth having.

***

I spent some time at a small private equity fund looking for new investments. My days passed with me sifting through marketing material from business brokers - flyers, pitchbooks (PowerPoint printouts), and financial statements - looking for a company interesting enough to show to my bosses. They told me the standard things: They wanted a cash generating machine in a good industry. I was familiar with that. **But then they also told me that they wanted a company selling for the right reasons.** As we are evaluating OpCo's buyout attractiveness, it helps also to step back for a minute and do a sanity check on the buyout candidate. Think about the question: Why now? Why should we purchase this company as it is at this period of time?

This is especially important to consider if OpCo is a privately owned family company. The founding family, having held onto the shares for many generations, now wants to sell. Why now? What do they know? The best thing to do now is to check out the owners and figure out why they are selling. More often than not they give the generic answer: "<u>The founding family seeks to diversify their financial wealth away from their company</u>."

It basically means **nothing**. Portfolio diversification tends to be a wonderful excuse to hide behind because it has become such an ingrained part of investing that people are almost afraid to argue against it. Yet the reasoning does not survive close scrutiny. If you are an owner of a fine business, there is no reason to sell a stake in that business - especially a controlling portion of it, which is much more valuable than just one measly share - for the sole sake of diversification. Owning a lot of one great company beats owning a whole lot of mediocre ones. So diversification makes no sense ... unless the company is not really that great of a company. And you want to get out while the going is good. The family, as managers, know this long before any analytic can because the accounting system is nowhere near as accurate as that employed by a public company.

What can be done? HTT digs in and does their research. **The founding family is always going to know more than the potential buyer, but circumstances do matter.** An aging patriarch looking to cash out after many years of running his company - that's a helpful step in the right direction. If the family is willing to help make a smooth transition or retains a minority stake that is another strong sign. If some of the family members or the entire family itself is engulfed in some crippling inter-familial conflict and has to cash out now, then that is another great sign (though one should never wish family strife on a clan - it is bad karma). What this firm wants is some indicator that the sale is not prompted by a very shrewd move to bail out of a sinking ship.

One of Warren Buffett's largest purchases is of the long-private industrial conglomerate Marmon Group, owned by the famous Pritzker family. After the family's patriarch, Jay Pritzker, died, the family embroiled itself in a vicious fight over the division up his powerful $15 billion business empire, which includes the famous Hyatt Hotels. As the family carved up the estate, Buffett stepped in and scooped up Marmon Group, closing a multi-year transition that keeps the family involved to enhance their own incentives and also make sense of the company's byzantine structure. Leave it to Buffett to make an *awesome* private equity type buyout.

There are a lot of private equity funds that buy small family owned businesses, fix them up, and then sell them. They often have to read the lines between the marketing text, establish a good relationship with the seller (often a rough and tumble entrepreneur type who cannot be bothered with suits and Wall Street types), and then build the company into a profitable money making machine. These funds tend to be on the smaller side, but their day-in-day-out business can get very good for them.

***

To some extent, you can say that the way HTT is thinking about their investment is the reverse of how the mindset is in a hedge fund. An analyst at your average hedge fund investing in long and short stocks sees a company's price and asks himself, "Wonder what price this can be?" Then he does research on the industry, studies possible investment events, and builds a model on Excel, usually a discounted cash flow model, so that he can predict where the stock price is going to be.

Private equity investing is different. Usually the price is already decided for the private equity analyst. If the company is public, then the analyst looks up the price and adds a premium. If the company is private then management has probably already hinted at an acceptable price. The essential question is not "Wonder what this price can be?" but instead, "How much return can we get if the price is this or that?"

Even the Excel models that the two analysts would use reflect this philosophical divergence. Hedge fund analysts analyze their investments with a discounted cash flow model or a DCF. The DCF takes in its builder's predictions and spits out a price. If the price by the model is much higher than that seen on the ticker, then the analyst can say that in time the price will go up to the model's expectation. A private equity analyst doing LBO work would not build a discounted cash flow but instead a <u>leveraged buyout model</u>. It is a different animal that requires you to first provide it with a buyout price. Then the model gives you a predicted return, which is what the analyst hopes the firm can get if everything turns out according to plan. So as you can see the two models are very different. One's entire purpose is to spit out a price. The other cannot start without a price.

***

The time period up to and during the LBO is pretty exciting. There is a lot of hustle and bustle. Press releases go flying out the door and columnists give their two cents on what this deal means for the economy at large. Once the deal is closed, the firm's employees are exhausted; it feels like they had just moved heaven and earth to get this company taken off the public markets and under the fund's wings.

However, their ordeal has just begun. The buyout just gets the ball rolling on the private equity investment process. **Now the fund has to get started on actually making the buyout profitable for the LPs and itself.** It is a huge difference between neatly modeling out "operational improvements" on an Excel spreadsheet and actually going onto the factory floor and making them happen in reality. The margin for error is razor thin; a debt-laden Sword of Damocles hangs over their heads by a thread.

So let's follow along with our protagonists. Next chapter!

Creating Value at OpCo

Now that the LBO is done, what next?

This is the longest single section in the book so be forewarned. My goal here is to tell you the story of how HTT makes its investment in OpCo a roaring success. Such a tale is going to look very chaotic at times so I have the graphic below to help you follow as things happen:

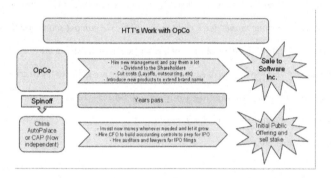

So as you see, HTT has a very simple plan. It is simple because OpCo is a great buy. As I detailed in the last section, OpCo is an ideal private equity investment. The core business generates a lot of cash and operates in a steady, mature industry. Also hidden inside the company's bowels is a unique subsidiary, a Chinese auto part retailer. These tenets make up HTT's investment thesis for the company and now the firm is in a position where it can unlock that value for the benefit of its investors and itself.

Here is the broad outline of the plan. The very first thing HTT is going to do is **have the old management leave and hire a new C-suite executive** to run the place. Then they will **split the company** in a unique transaction called a spinoff, which results in the Chinese retailer being a separate company of its own. The example then follows the two sister companies as they grow and develop. Their different circumstances mean that different things are going to have to be done.

With the original OpCo, HTT is going to make the company **pay out a dividend to its owners, HTT itself.** Why they want to do this you will learn is to make sure that the fund's LPs can *get some money back right now and the GP can get sooner paid its incentive fees.* Next, HTT **cuts costs** by offshoring some costs, laying off workers, and selling whatever they do not need. At the same time, they are going to try to grow the company's revenues by **introducing some new products.** These are standard consulting type recommendations (and indeed a lot of the PE people overseeing this process are former consultants).

Let's continue. Here we go!

***

Day after the deal is sealed: *HTT has presciently negotiated for themselves and OpCo management a massive buyout of their contracts. The former CEO and board of directors take their money to Rio and their own private islands. Now it's time to bring in some top executive talent. They call up someone at GE or some other place with a great reputation for developing executive talent and offer them the perks of running a*

191

company out of the public spotlight. More compellingly they also offer a titanic amount of stock if they do it right. The New Guy will get paid a hell of a lot of money but if he makes money for the GPs and the LPs then one can argue that the money was well spent.

HTT, now in full control of OpCo, takes a deep dive into the company. It is more than likely that they have long ago planned out what to do, with detailed goals to hit and deliverables to deliver. They comb the financials and walk the sales floors with the salesmen. They hire expensive consultants from prestigious firms to explore new ideas for improving the company.[48] After evaluating the private financials - things like profit per unit of software and subsidiary growth - they realize that there are certain actions that they can take that will immediately reward themselves and their partners.

You may be surprised to know that multi-millionaire and billionaire private equity partners have troubles keeping them up at night, but indeed they do. HTT serves its clients, and operates at its clients' pleasure. And their clients are always asking, "So uhh ... when are we going to get our money back?" The reality is that they are not going to get all of it back until the company is entirely sold off. That liquidation event as it is called is probably years away into the future. What can be done right now? That answer is a dividend, a debt-fueled dividend.

---

[48] Some private equity funds have their own in-house stable of consultants who they can rely on to create value out of their investments. It becomes a great selling point to tell your potential LPs that your unique murderers' row of consultants are smarter and more engaged than any outside firm can ever be. After all, there are real issues with listening to the advice of a consultant who is being paid regardless of how his projects turn out.

A company generates profit for its shareholders. **If that company has some excess profit that it does not know what to do with, management has the option of paying that money to the shareholders through a dividend.** For most companies, dividends are paid out of profits generated from operations. A company has a very successful year, realizes it has made more money than it immediately needs, and rewards the shareholders by paying it to them. The shareholders like that and buy more of the stock. Everyone wins.

HTT has a dual role in OpCo as **both shareholder and management**. Thus it is in the unique position of being able to pay itself by having the company declare a dividend. Money flows out of the company right to the shareholders. Limited partners in the fund get some of their money back. However such a move is not made just because HTT is feeling charitable towards its investors. There is an ulterior motive.

At the same time, the GP inches closer towards getting paid an incentive fee. Remember what I said about incentive fees? They are only charged if the LP's money starts to grow. Let us say an LP puts in $10 towards this OpCo deal. **HTT is free to charge them management fee on that $10, but they cannot charge an incentive fee on that $10. No, they can only charge that nice 20% incentive once the OpCo deal earns that eleventh dollar.** Applying one of the core concepts to this situation, HTT has to break the high water mark before they can charge the incentive fee. The high water mark is $10. That first dollar past $10, HTT gets 20 cents. So HTT wants to get them that $10 and fast. If they can get a dividend first out of OpCo and reach that $10 sooner ... well then so much the better. Imagine if HTT can reach that $10 threshold just through dividends. They still have not sold or IPO'ed the company yet! And since a sale or IPO is usually where the most money is made, it means a very fat incentive fee coming for the GP.

Truth is that it is unlikely that OpCo has enough free cash lying around to pay that much in dividend. After all, if the company's operations were generating that much cash then they probably would have not needed to go private in the first place. **So where is this dividend money coming from if not operations? The answer is that HTT borrows it from the debt markets.** It makes OpCo issue a whole lot more junk bonds into the debt market so that it can take that money and hand it right on over to the shareholders. It is kind of similar to people taking out a home equity line of credit except that you have not really started to build any equity yet.

It is not a move well received by the media, who would prefer that the company spend it on making the business better. I probably would not put it in the personal finance hall of fame either. But if the debt markets buy those junk bonds then that means that somebody out there believes that HTT knows something that most people do not. As management insiders they have access to every piece of information regarding the health and potential of the company's business. If the metrics imply that the company can handle the additional debt load then why not pay the shareholders? If you are looking for people to blame, blame the bond markets as well for it is them who decide that the company is worth giving another couple million. It takes two to tango. These debt dividends were pretty common in the mid 2000s with some of the mega-buyouts and all the easy money flying around. I have not heard of them so much after the bond markets froze up in 2008. They either stopped making such deals or they are just not as public with them anymore.

***

Building Value: *OpCo is not a cutting edge organization pushing the borders of innovation and imagination like a Groupon or a Facebook. OpCo is a large company working in a very mature field, meaning that all the crazy growth is gone. Growth has its own strategies for management - we will save that for OpCo's crazy growing little subsidiary. For OpCo's core business there is an accumulation of literature with very specific strategies - a doctor's prescription for a cachet of drugs.*

HTT grimly rolls up their sleeves and dives into the messy business of improving the health of the business. Layoffs, outsourcing, closing plants. There is a lot of unpleasantness that needs to be dealt with. As a private company, it can do these things without constantly being under the public company spotlight. It helps a little bit to make the job easier.

But HTT would not have gone as far as it did if all they brought to a company was a set of butcher knives. Private equity firms come armed with a wealth of contacts. It is one of their strongest traits. If a partner at HTT realizes that a contact in the Rolodex can help further OpCo's ultimate goals, then they will not hesitate to do so. New business, smart executive talent, whatever is needed can be brought in by OpCo's new owners.

The hard work pays off and OpCo reports a very high profit in the year after the buyout. HTT cut a lot of redundant costs but also brought in new operating procedures that allowed company salesmen more leeway to offer discounts and other retaining offers to customers. The result is that sales to companies stayed strong and picked up steam as the economy turns for the better. One of HTT's other private equity companies specialized in web software, so the two enterprises worked together to release a web version of OpCo's business software, offering it to ordinary folks at a reasonable price. The new product is a huge hit and grows OpCo revenues.

What a PE firm is going to do with an individual portfolio company changes depending on the situation. **Sometimes a fund is going to tell you that they have a standard playbook that they are going to use with their investments, a book where you can look up the exact problem and find its time-tested solution.** If they think that the company competes in a field where everyone is just stealing customers from each other, they cut some costs and boost advertising to get the word out. If they think the brand would be recognized in foreign countries then they go overseas and sell their wares there. If they think there is a similar market to which they can extend the brand, then they build a new product to take advantage. These are the types of solutions that a playbook would offer. It makes strategy planning a fill-in-the-blank exercise.

So does such a playbook exist? Yes it does and I have seen it (saying that made me feel like Indiana Jones or something). Is it all that special and does it always work? No.

How successful those strategic overtures are depend on, like with any business venture, the validity and execution of the concept.

Execution and concept is always important but it is especially crucial with a company like OpCo. First is the competition. The market is not growing fast enough to make everyone successful so the only way you can win by making others lose. If stuff goes wrong, then you become the cold corpse people step over on their way to success. And then there is the debt load. Yes one can definitely argue that debt focuses a company and lights a fire under their seats to really go out there and succeed. At the same time it leaves no margin for error and makes people a little afraid to innovate.

Things are a lot easier in a big booming industry or a big booming economy. All that growth means that there is enough space for all the fish in the pond. When your industry has a lot of room to run and the big players have not yet been established, it is kind of hard to mess up. Everybody looks like a genius. And indeed with China AutoPalace people are about to look very smart.

China AutoPalace - Spinoff and Massive Growth: *Several years ago, one of OpCo's early employees left to start a small company selling automobile inventory management software in China. OpCo purchased the small company for a pittance several years later and simply ignored it. The small company, called China AutoPalace or CAP, eventually expanded into a new business selling auto repair parts to consumers at a series of retail stores in large Chinese cities like Sichuan and Guangdong. These are cities with millions of people, many of getting being lifted out of poverty by the booming the Chinese economy. They get cars and drive around. When*

197

their cars break down, CAP provides a convenient place to get replacement parts. CAP's revenues are small but they are growing fast, and the company has a bright future.

HTT cuts CAP out of OpCo and makes it its own separate company in a process financial types call a spinoff. The situation is a boon for both parties. OpCo can fully focus on rebuilding the core business software business, CAP gets to grow from out under the yoke of a clueless parent, and the shareholders win most of all because (as explained in an earlier chapter) spinoffs are unusually strong drivers of shareholder wealth. HTT pours additional capital into the new company and CAP's grows its revenues and profits at an astounding rate. The internal valuation experts brought in to measure the value of HTT's investments note that CAP is a real winner, and gives the company a high multiple.[49] The LPs are pleased.

***

We are **halfway** through our example so I want to take a look back at our graphic and just re-emphasize some of the concepts I went over:

---

[49] Companies on Wall Street are valued as according to multiples of a certain performance figure. This means that you can calculate the full value of a company by taking this multiplying factor and applying to the cited accounting figure. The one usually cited is EBITDA - earnings before interest, taxes, and depreciation / amortization - a very long term that is a rough proxy for "cash flow" or basically how much cash the company is throwing off every year. Saying ten times EBITDA means that you can get the full value of the company by looking up EBITDA and multiplying by 10. It's a good way to adjust for a company's size. A big company might on the surface cost more than a small one simply because its EBITDA is higher, but if the multiples are identical, then they are essentially being valued equally.

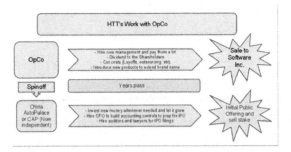

HTT refreshed its managers and then **brought in some new blood**. By paying them a whole lot of money, the PE firm convinces them to try their best (I would work very hard too for many millions of dollars). Then it **spun off** the exciting Chinese auto-retailing subsidiary (called China AutoPalace).

After that, HTT **paid itself** a dividend. It was able to find the money to do so by selling some more debt into the debt markets. In doing this they get two things out of it: 1) The LPs get some of their money back immediately, and 2) The GP gets a little closer to breaking their <u>high water mark</u> and getting paid the true big bucks, the incentive fees.

Satiated, HTT came up with a series of strategic steps to make the company a contender. They slimmed down by **laying off personnel** and **outsourcing work**. Then they **introduced new products** that consumers wanted and resulted in revenue growth. Profits the next year were very encouraging.

Starting with the next paragraph, I am going to discuss HTT selling OpCo to a competitor and why might it would want to do that. **Probably the most important**

detail I can tell you pay attention to in that section is the difference between a strategic and financial buyer. The issue was a hugely topical one in the boom boom private equity years from 2004-2007.

Once OpCo is sold off, I am going to finish the example by telling you about what HTT does with CAP. To spare the suspense they are going to IPO the business but the important thing to learn here is **why** they want to and **the steps they need to take** to pull it off.

***

After the successful spinoff, HTT now has two companies on its hands. As both these companies grow and improve within the PE portfolio the partners now have to deal with a new situation.

The biggest question that every PE group asks before it gets into an investment is how on earth they are going to get out of it. If a company is the right size then they can sell it to a larger company, sell it to another private equity firm, or go IPO and put it on the public markets. By and large, this is pretty much it and if the investment is a super large company then pretty much the only way to go is IPO.

(That being said, you should never discount a PE firm's creativity. KKR liquidated RJR Nabisco by selling off the fruit division, spinning off the cigarette division, taking another part public, using RJR stock as payment for another LBO later on, and then selling the rest off nearly 15 years later.)

This exit strategy dilemma applies to both OpCo and CAP but let us first focus on OpCo. Fortunately for HTT, OpCo is at the right size for being acquired. It does business in a field full of very large fish, and those fish would be pleased to have the opportunity to tack on OpCo's business software offerings to their own. HTT decides that they are not going to IPO OpCo but instead try to sell the company to a competitor. It gets the company off their books immediately and they do not have to go through the trouble and hassle of preparing for an IPO.

***

Selling OpCo to Software Inc.: *OpCo has been through the wringer, and the company that remains is sleek and efficient. The sales team is top notch and the new web suite is a real hit. The company has been private for several years but now it is time to exit the investment and bring the limited partners their returns. HTT decides that they want to try to find a strategic buyer, a company who sees the worth in having OpCo as part of their company and their strategic plan going forward, thus the reason for the name.*

They hire an investment bank to shop the company to any potential clients. One large company, Software Inc., is intrigued by OpCo's many attractive features. The investment bank arranges a meeting between HTT and Software Inc, and before long they strike a deal that pays a good price. The LPs get an impressive return on their investment and the investment bank gets a hefty fee for their trouble.

As I mentioned above, there are two types of buyers. There are strategic buyers and financial buyers.

A financial buyer is another private equity firm, a fellow denizen of Wall Street. They intend to buy the company from HTT so that they can "fix it up" once more. **It is a transaction that basically means that OpCo goes through the same fun and games that HTT just ran them through.** The only difference is that the new financial buyer thinks that they can do it better. If it reminds you of back during the housing boom days when a person would buy a house, never live in it, and then flip it a few months later to another schlepp intending to do the same, you are not dreaming. It indeed is pretty much what is going on.

PE to PE transactions were more common before the financial bubble as the financing was easy to get and funds were never so powerful as they were then. The financial crisis pretty much ended the practice. The funding all dried up. Who would want to lend money to someone who wants to buy and flip? **Echoing the sentiment, the largest, most important LPs made it clear that they were against the practice.** This is because more often than not they would have investments in funds from both the buying and selling PE groups. So from their perspective the invested company just went from one part of their portfolio to the other. The investor is made no better for the wear and in fact is worse off because of all the fees that were incurred. During the financial crisis the power shifted away from the private equity groups so the LPs had their way and the practice has now for the most part ended.

Strategic buyers are more much amenable. Oracle and AT&T are examples of companies who frequently acquire companies with the intention of keeping it towards achieving their future plans. They operate in industries that have matured and are no longer growing as fast. **Since the customers are getting saturated with product and there are no more to convert, one of the few remaining options for these large companies to maintain their previous growth is to buy another company in that same space.** This way, they add the purchased company's old customers, can squeeze profit from economies of scale (cutting costs and sharing duties), or acquire some new product that compliments their current offering. These buyers are not going to flip their purchase so they can pay more than a financial buyer, who wants a price that lets them make a profit.

***

OpCo is now successfully sold, but what about CAP? Under HTT's ownership China AutoPalace has become a runaway star in HTT's portfolio. **The company makes billions in revenue a year and its owners know more is coming, as CAP is located right in the maw of several massive supercells of growth**: Chinese economy, a rising middle class, and automobile retailing. With so many hot investing keywords in one place, there is no question that the line of buyers piling up to take CAP off HTT's hands would stretch around the block like on iPad day at the San Francisco Apple store.

Even so, a sale would cause a real riot amongst the LPs. If HTT sold CAP off to someone else they would be cheating themselves of the company's future phenomenal growth.

Yet there is no point of having a huge uncut diamond jangling in your pocket if you cannot turn it into money to buy food for your kids. They cannot hold CAP forever. The best way, then, to have your cake and eat it too is to take the company public and put the stock on the trading floor. Once the company is public, HTT can sell the shares off whenever it is prudent to produce money to return to the partners.

In addition, HTT has decided that the moment is right for an IPO. The stock markets are frothy with excess cash and they are looking for something to invest with it. Investors also have "hot" and "not" sectors in which they are itching to buy into. A few years ago it was the tech bubble (AOL and Cisco), few years after that it was energy (oil and ... oil). Right now, it seems like China has been on the lips of all the big investors. They really want the next big China play and HTT is going to give it to them. On the IPO day, it is likely that the price will soar.

China AutoPalace - IPO and Champagne: *Though it is a relief that a decision has been made regarding HTT's rising star, there remains much work to do. For a long time, CAP has been literally ignored by its owners, who did not want to mess with a good thing. However a public company needs to live up to certain standards to be worth looking at by investors, especially the big institutional ones that really buy shares in bulk. CAP is no longer a tiny startup. The diamond in HTT's pocket is huge, but it needs to be cut, polished, and shined by an artisan.*

HTT gives CAP's management money and expertise to set up a system to record their sales, share data, and track inventory. Using their contacts, the private equity firm also brings in a CFO, who works to improve the balance sheet and bring the company's financial management skills up to par with that expected of a public company. He engages an auditor and a law firm to prepare the documents necessary for an IPO.

Once the documents are completed, the company calls forth an investment bank to arrange the big day. Together with CAP management, everyone goes out on a road show to drum up excitement from all the important institutional investors. They are all very excited and just as expected the share offering is "oversubscribed." This means that investors have put in orders for more shares of stock than what is being offered. The result is a price that must go higher.

On IPO day, the shares begin trading on the Hong Kong stock markets and it is a huge hit. A frantic day of trading amongst the institutional investors begins as savvy investors take profits on the rising stock price. HTT watches the company's skyrocketing value and is now able to use it to value the shares they currently have in the portfolio. Once regulations allow them to sell those shares several months down the line, the firm will be able to hand back to their investors (and themselves) a whole lot of money. The partners bring out a bottle of champagne. Good job, everyone!

***

Here my example closes. The returns on a private equity investment vary depending on the quality of the thesis and how well it runs after the buyout happens. A good deal can return up to two or three times the invested capital. These returns are highly valued especially when you remember that it gets harder and harder to generate high returns when you have more money. **This is why pension funds love PE despite all of pitfalls - they successfully grow huge amounts of money.**

The OpCo-CAP example was, as you probably expect, very optimistic. Few investments run as smoothly or are as successful as the one HTT just pulled. Yet I did not make the whole thing up. In 1984, KKR performed a leveraged buyout of a company called Malone and Hyde. Several years later they spun off a small auto retailing subsidiary called AutoShack (later to be AutoZone). The company prospered and in 1991 the PE firm took them public. By the time KKR divested the last of its AutoZone shares in 1999, the partners had made back their investment many times over. It was a phenomenal investing success built on the two pillars of private equity success: **Good operating skills combined with the patience of Job.**

Private Equity Outside of LBOs

How do PE firms make money if they are not doing LBOs?

In the last section I wove together a massive walkthrough of the leveraged buyout. It is a huge undertaking that involves a lot of money and just as much patience. Unfortunately, this is the part of the book where I tell you that these things do not happen so much anymore. Why? The truth is that a gigantic leveraged buyout only happens when there are banks and other organizations willing to lend money to the HTTs of the world to execute their buyouts. When that credit dries up then so do the really big buyouts. That is exactly what happened after the financial crash in 2008. The last truly big buyout happened in 2007 when Blackstone Group bought Hilton Hotels (yes, Paris Hilton. That Hilton.) for $26 billion. Today's banks are much less willing to lend out their money because both the deals they made in the boom-boom years did not always do well and they are simply more conservative. To get a sense of this new type of funding environment, in 2013 Silver Lake Partners - a rare big private equity firm that works exclusively in tech - made a $24 billion deal for Dell, the computer company. In order to round up all the money they needed to buy all of the company's shares, they had to get $13.75 billion in loans from Bank of America, Barclays, Credit Suisse, and RBC[50]. But

[50] You can read more about the structure of this deal in the 8K filed to the SEC.

http://www.sec.gov/Archives/edgar/data/826083/000119312513041273/d480506d8k.htm

that is still short so they need $2 billion from Microsoft - not a bank, but a rich strategic partner. Then they got some $500 million from Michael Dell himself, who would also throw all of his shares - 16% of the company - into the deal for practically nothing. So to recap, in order to get a 2007-type deal going in 2013, Silver Lake had to have a founder who still owns a large amount of the company to contribute his shares, bring in four banks from across the world to make loans, and nab a wealthy "strategic partner" with cash to burn to put in money of its own. (And as of Aug 2013, the deal still has not been closed because there are people saying that the price is not enough!) That is a lot of cats to herd for a deal that would barely rank in the Top 10 biggest LBOs ever. So in other words, the mega-LBO age is for now over.

So if private equity groups - and only a few dozen out of the hundreds out there in the world - are not executing these buyouts, then what are they doing?

In an earlier section of this book, I wrote about hedge funds making private equity type investments or side-pockets. There, hedge funds go to small, private companies with a lot of potential and strike deals with them. The company gets a whole lot of money to expand or pursue some strategic initiative while the hedge fund gets an investment that no other fund can boast of having. **However, hedge funds are a terrible vehicle for these investments** because of illiquidity issues and I wrote of an ill-fated example. Smaller private equity funds, though, fit the bill perfectly. A private equity fund has the right personnel - armed with the right experience and patience - to go and make these deals. More importantly, their investors are prepared to wait just as long to get their money back.

This is a different type of private equity investment in that it does not take on leverage. It does not mean, however, that there is a lot less risk in the portfolio. In fact it may still be just as risky. When you are investing in smaller companies that may be operating in foreign countries or unpredictable industries such as biomedicine, then it is possible that an unfortunate turn of events can cause the fledgling company to collapse and the investor to lose all of his investment. A huge buyout target like OpCo has a lot of resilience from its sheer size, there are options that a private equity fund can explore if things are not going to plan. For a tiny company, it is sink or swim.

As a result of this risk, the investing private equity firm is going to demand from its partner some protections. This means owning some sort of bond, because owning debt gives you certain privileges that stockholders cannot themselves demand. Yet at the same time, the firm wants to have the opportunity to get rich if the company does very well and becomes a roaring success. That means owning some sort of stock, because equity holders are entitled to all the profits that a company can earn. It seems like a contradiction does it not? **They want upside potential ... but they also want protection too.** You cannot have your cake and eat it too right? Wrong. The magic of finance has created a series of cross-dressing bond-stock hybrids[51] that bestow upon its owner all the benefits of both worlds. These securities (which include convertible bonds, preferred stock, and mezzanine debt) are probably some of the best investments an investor can get.

---

[51] I talk a lot more about these in the section on bonds.

These minority stake type private equity deals are also common for groups operating foreign countries. Such stakes can be astoundingly profitable even without the magic of leverage. You can learn a lot more about foreign private equity investing in its respective section coming up soon.

***

You can make a private equity style minority investment in a public company too. Such a thing is called a **PIPE or Private Investments in Public Entities**. Here is how it works. There is a struggling company, Wooden Corp. Let us say they make furniture. They find themselves in a bit of a slump and miss earning expectations for a several consecutive quarters. The stock drops like a dead pigeon and the debt markets become less willing to lend to the company. Wooden need to pay the workers and the suppliers, and if you run out of money then you have to file for bankruptcy. **Management realizes that the bond markets will charge such exorbitant rates that the company will slowly bleed to death.** They need to get money through alternate means.

Here arrives HTT, fresh off their home run success with OpCo. They have heard about Wooden's recent issues. The market may be jittery about lending to Wooden but after doing some research the private equity firm believes that if the company can make it through their temporary financing issues then business will rebound with the economy. HTT offers Wooden a deal. **In exchange for locking up their money with Wooden for a long time, HTT receives a special security with preferential treatment.** It is just like the bond-stock hybrid securities of which I just gone over in the last section, it provides for its owner downside protections - interest payments along with a greater claim to assets than common shareholders - while also providing the unlimited upside benefit of equity. The security is one of a kind - it cannot be bought from the market. It must be created by its originator, and that nature is what makes it a private equity style investment.

The arrangement allows the fund to acquire a large stake in a public company without having to go through the public markets. Trying to buy the same number of stock through the markets causes the price to rise and may put it out of the investor's comfort zone.

Unfortunately what is good for this one investor is usually not so for the rest of them. **This is because the PIPE investor has many downside protections to protect their influence in the company's matters at the cost of ordinary retail investors who just bought plain common stock.** If the public company continues to struggle and sells new stock to raise money, HTT's stake would normally be diluted from the new flood of shares onto the market. This is mathematics; a larger denominator of total shares equals a smaller fraction of your own personal shares. Every previous stakeholder sees their percentage ownership of the company decline. A PIPE can prevent this by happening by forcing the company to issue HTT enough free shares so that their ownership percentage does not change. Essentially if the denominator must rise, then so should the PIPE's numerator. This is good for HTT but it hurts everyone else because their own unprotected stakes shrink even further.

The frequency with which PIPEs are made is correlated to the ease with which a company can raise funds on their own from the capital markets. **If interest rates are at a low and junk bonds at selling at record high prices (thus giving record low yields) then companies would rather issue a mass of junk bonds than infuriate their current shareholders by making sweetheart deals with loan sharks in nice suits.** In fact if Wooden is smart, they add some sort of exit clause into the investment contract so that when those low interest rates finally do come around for them, they can raise money and buy the debt back from its owners. While this would be a displeasing development for HTT because they lose out on the money they could have gotten by holding it to maturity, the firm would undoubtedly make Wooden pay extra to exit their contract. That buyout amount would have to do.

***

I have studied a lot of private equity groups and especially the larger ones. The majority of their portfolios are made up on investments based on the three models of which I just reviewed in this section and the last: Buyout, minority investment in private companies, and PIPEs. So if you powered through their respective sections then you have just built a pretty thorough understanding of how the private equity investing model works.

But before you shut this book and head on over to that copy of *Twilight*, I have here a few more chapters on certain nuances of the business that I found interesting. Private equity is a fascinating subject because there is so much more to the industry that one can think about beyond just the investments. Having had a lot of experience dealing with private equity and hedge fund clients and on the fund marketing side, I found those parts just as fascinating as the deal making. New developments both exciting and troubling are happening in the industry as we speak. Such things, of which you can learn more about in the next chapters, include foreign private equity, the rise of "secondary markets", and the private equity firms owning hedge funds.

So I highly encourage you to turn the page. We are not finished yet ...

Beyond the Investing

On funds, their clients, and the industry at large

Over the past few sections we talked about the basics. Things like 1) What a hedge fund is, 2) What is the difference between LPs and GPs, 3) How fees are earned and paid, 4) Who the LPs are and what they want, and 5) What are the risks of investing in private equity funds.

Now that we are through with this basic stuff, I can start raising the gates a little and discuss some other aspects of fund relationship management and marketing. If I am going too fast, do not worry. You can always come back. With my teaching style - **you are going to see these concepts repeated again and again. Because learning something is hard and it takes time and multiple exposures.**

This large section looks at the sometimes testy relationship between a private equity fund and its clients. It is more of an issue simply because of the nature of the industry; your money is locked up for years. The private equity firm might be patient enough to grin and bear it but the LPs might not (especially when they are not getting paid nice 2% management fees). Each section here is going to try to answer a question regarding the GP-LP relationship:

~ How are private equity funds structured and how is that different from hedge funds?

~ What if an LP wants out before a fund is ready to return money to its investors?

~ What can a private equity fund add as an added bonus to woo a potential investor?

~ What are some pensions funds doing that is worrying some private equity groups?

These are topics that I wanted to write about but found required some familiarity with the model and its players before introducing. Yes it may be at times confusing but if you have been following along alright then you are going to catch on pretty quickly.

***

Investing in a private equity fund is kind of like sending your kids off to college. They disappear for years and you fret over their health and well-being the whole time they are gone. It is definitely a long term exercise in patience with both parties getting intimately acquainted with each other. It is also like one of those love-hate romantic comedies. (You can tell that I am a fan of bad metaphors.) **In this section I want to go into some of a private equity firm's operations and how it runs and allocates deals between its funds as well as the reason for doing it this way.**

Did you know that hedge funds and private equity funds raise and structure their funds differently? Hedge funds are most often set up as a sort of rolling stone. People can jump in and out but the rolling stone rolls on indefinitely or at least until there are no more people to move the stone further on. Theoretically, the fund can last forever. Renaissance Technologies' Medallion Fund and George Soros' Quantum Fund have been chugging for decades now. Long as there is money in the fund, the fund will live on.

A private equity fund has a definite end point. If HTT raises a fund of $5 billion dollars, they will use that money to make investments of all the types that are available to PE firms - LBOs, PIPEs, and more. They raise a fund by signing contracts with LPs and are promised a certain amount of money from the LP. When the money is finally needed for investing, HTT sends their LPs a capital call instructing the money to be promptly wired into their bank account. The LPs now must pay up or else they default. The money is used and slowly HTT builds up a portfolio of its private equity investments. Years pass and the investments are turned back into cash either through IPOs or sales. The money does not get rolled into the fund but instead it is sent back to the LPs. Once the last investment is turned into cash, the fund disappears. This could take a very long time, decades even if the firm decides that it is worth it to hold for that long. KKR held Primedia, a media firm, for 22 years from beginning to end.

As a result of this long lived farm-like structure, **mega sized private equity firms, like our hypothetical one here, raise and tend to many different funds in addition to a huge flagship fund.** Kind of like in a yogurt shop, each fund has their own flavor. If some LP wants a fund that has an investment focus in Asia because they think Asian markets are the way to go, then HTT might have an Asian fund of some size.

If an LP wants a fund geared exclusively towards Technology, then HTT might have one there too. If the LP has no idea what they want to do, then they might just put their money into the titanic flagship fund, the largest fund and the one people will most often bring up in the conversation.[52] It all depends on the specific allocation to which they wish to overweight.

When I first heard of this setup, I had thought that each one of these funds are siloed off from each other. A firm creates competing funds with their own teams and lets them fight each other out in a sort of vicious Darwinian battle royale. It seems in line with what I assumed to be the Wall Street cut-throat nature. Maybe there are a few funds out there doing this but not the ones I have worked with. Too much discord and workplace politics and it leads to the best people leaving.

Instead, a deal is sourced, investigated, negotiated and closed. Then it is doled out to each fund in proportions. HTT bought 100% of OpCo. They will put the majority of the shares, maybe 50%, into HTT Capital Appreciation III, their newest flagship fund. But they will also put 30% into the HTT Asian Fund, because of the random Chinese car part subsidiary. And 10% into the HTT Technology fund, because OpCo makes software. They use pretty broad guidelines in deciding what goes where. One would be surprised to see many overlaps between the "Asian Fund" and the "European Fund".

---

[52] None for dealing with confusing new naming schemes, the partners will often name their flagships after themselves and then tack on a Roman numeral for every new one they manage to raise (i.e. HTT can offer their valued investors HTT Capital Appreciation Fund I, HTT Capital Apprecation Fund II, and so on).

So why should you care for all of these different types of funds? I have two things here and they are both related to how times have changed since the early private equity years.

***

First, the different number of funds allows for a **dilution effect between all of them**. Times have changed since KKR bought RJR Nabisco. Even though KKR did not have to pay the whole price out of their fund, the down payment they plunked for it was still a sizable chunk of their current flagship fund. **So they put themselves in a situation where the firm's overall performance is going to depend a lot on whether or not the RJ investment works out.** If you recall what I wrote earlier then you know RJR did not turn out to be the winner they imagined it to be. HTT avoids walking the same tightrope that KKR did by seeding their deals across all their funds. Assuming that their LPs are not invested in every fund the firm offers, the brunt of any losses is dispersed across the many LPs in all the firm's offered funds.[53]

Another thing that is different about the RJR deal (as well as this HTT example) is that the PE firm took out the entire company on its own. This is because they were the only firm who could punch hard enough to take on the deal. Today this is no longer the case and HTT would find many identically sized firms in its space. They all compete for deals and more often than not once a good potential deal is found there is usually another firm wanting in too. After all, OpCo would be an idiot not to shop around to all the possible suitors.

---

[53] Hedge funds do this too if they have multiple funds. There may be a dozen or so funds but only three or four truly differentiated strategies.

Rather than doing an all-or-nothing or sparking off an eBay auction situation, the two firms would probably end up splitting the deal between themselves. HTT provides 50% of the equity down payment and PE firm number 2 the other half. The very large deals that happened in the mid to late 2000s had many different PE groups participating. So there is a second dilution effect as well, one working between firms in addition to the one that happens within a single firm between its many funds. For example, the massive LBO of hospital operator HCA in 2006 cost $31.6 billion. The deal was headed by Bain Capital, KKR, and Merrill Lynch's private equity division. In other words, three big funds who probably share a lot of investors. A large institutional investor who is invested in multiple funds offered by many firms could go through their annual reports and note a bunch overlapping investments by different firms.

This practice does lead to some problems. Institutional investors want to know that their funds are not all investing in the same thing. If they are, then why invest in so many? In addition, having so many parties at the punch bowl means it is harder to bring in changes to company operations. It is a simple common sense. Nobody appreciates a backseat driver and having half a dozen of them puts too many cooks in the kitchen. After the financial crash, these club deals disappeared not only because of funding for them disappeared but also because the big LPs put a stop to it.

***

The second "reason" is more intriguing in that I am not even sure if it is a real reason. It is just something that I have overheard but it sure makes me think. It is about the splintering of the product line which is a tactic used often by businesses selling new products. Look below for how it works.

When Apple introduced the iPod in 2002 or whenever, there was only 1 type of iPod. It played music, was white in color, and had a nice click wheel. The company grew rapidly behind the fortunes of this single iPod and the growth was so good that supply could barely keep up with demand. Things were good. But then it so happened that after a few years the original iPod's growth began to falter. People loved the thing but now a lot of them owned it. How does Apple maintain the growth? By splintering the line. Apple introduced the iPod Mini, the iPod Color, the iPod Video, the Nano, and the Shuffle. By creating many different variations of the same product, Apple exploits previously untapped pockets of demand. It is a hassle to create and put into production so many different variants, so such an action can only be justified if the iPod's previous growth cannot be maintained with a single product.

Perhaps all these fund variants are a result of the same dynamic. For years KKR and Blackstone expanded their business while raising just one fund at a time and they were able to get away with it because the private equity industry was so young and growing in leaps and bounds. Then the growth began to falter and soon it became clear that just one "product" - the flagship fund - was not going to keep the company growing like it was before. So they splinter the "product" into many. They have European Funds, Asian Funds, and Technology Funds because they want to reach those investors who wanted those things and stayed out of the market because those niche funds were not being offered. Those niche funds are not even close to being as large as the big flagship funds and because they managed so much less money, good but small deals looked better in those portfolios. (Remember what I said about the law of managing more money? With billions of dollars to grow, you need to find not only great deals but BIG ones as well. Buffett has been complaining about it for years.)

I have no idea if it is the whole explanation but it is certainly an interesting theory. It makes sense because of one irrefutable fact: **American private equity is a mature industry.** It has been going along for nearly a quarter of a century. The crazy growth is gone. Remember when I was talking about OpCo and the special steps that HTT should take to make sure that an older company in a mature industry succeeds? Well the sentiment applies to HTT and its cohorts as well. These private equity firms are OpCos in a mature pond. This means they have to do things differently and execute well to make sure that the company succeeds against its competition and does not lose ground. What some of things are I will come to in some of the later sections.

***

So just now I worked through some aspects of a private equity firm's operations. I started by surveying the differences between a private equity fund and a hedge fund. A private equity fund has a life and an ending. A hedge fund generally goes on and on like the Energizer Bunny until its managers decide that they do not want to run it anymore.

Then I went into the multi-fund structures of these private equity funds. I talked about how these funds have so many different accents and focuses. These focuses can be by industry, geography or more. Then I gave two possible reasons for this split, which at first glance seems cosmetic: 1) Diversification, and 2) Adaptation to a maturing industry

Let us go back to the set of questions I posed in the first few paragraphs of this section.

~~**~ How are private equity funds structured and how is that different from hedge funds?**~~

~ What if an LP wants out before a fund is ready to return money to its investors?

~ What can a private equity fund add as an added bonus to woo a potential investor?

~ What are some pensions funds doing that is worrying some private equity groups?

The first has been addressed. For the other three, let us move on to the next section.

***

What if an LP wants out before the investments are ready?

It is often true that once an LP invests into a fund then they are locked in with that fund for a very long time. Once the money is sent and invested, the LP does not see it again for many years. **However it is possible to circumvent this multi-year lockup by selling your stake on a private, secondary market.** Think of it kind of like a divorce.

Once an LP decides that they want out of a private equity fund, there are a variety of ways to cement the separation. A variety of private secondary exchanges can grease the rails on a transaction. The process works kind of like an auction; participants indicate their interest and bid to a price. Once a winner emerges, the exchange helps facilitate the process for a percentage fee. You may have heard about these in the newspapers because it is there where a lot of private tech companies like Facebook and Twitter traded on for some time. But the exchanges can do the same for LPs of PE funds and other large partnerships - hedge fund investors expect that they can usually pull their money out of a fund on a relatively short basis.[54] A sale here is more difficult (and thus more expensive) to pull off than simply calling up a broker and clicking a button online but it does provide a way out for the unhappy private equity investor.

LPs do this because they need the money quickly, perhaps to pay some prominent stakeholder. Or if they think they are allocating too much money to this particular asset class. Or it could be also that the LP just wants out of a lagging fund. During the mid 2000s, PE groups raised some truly massive funds: Blackstone's Blackstone Capital Partners V, raised in 2006, was $21.7 billion large, Goldman Sachs Capital Partners VI, raised in 2007, was $20.3 billion large.[55] These are huge private equity funds, larger than a good 95% of the rest of the fund universe. Not only that but as you learned in the previous section these funds are just a few in a stable of many. A Blackstone Group or a

---

[54] Unless the hedge fund has dropped the gates on these "redemptions" as they are called. During 2008, hedge funds were so overwhelmed with redemptions they activated "lock up clauses," forcing LPs to stay in the fund as the stock market crashed. Needless to say, LPs were not pleased.
[55] I referred to Preqin for this information. Preqin is a company providing information on hedge funds and private equity.

Goldman Sachs has many more private equity funds (which are themselves billions of dollars large) in addition to the big flagship.

These funds are many times larger than what they used to be a decade and a half ago - up to four times as large. Has the economy grown at a equivalent pace? In 15 years, has the economy's growth kept up with the growth in the size of its private equity funds? It has not. Thus, the competition gets more intense. Intense competition forces down returns. **So knowing that, you can understand why people are skeptical that the funds can make money on that much money.** Even taking into account the bull market of 2009-2010, funds at best have clawed their way back to where they started - a 0% return. This calculates out to some disappointing five year returns.

But it is not even the past that the LPs are concerned about. Plenty of funds have had unsteady births only to go on to yield wildly successful harvests for their investors. It is more the future outlook of the portfolio companies. Many of these multi-billion dollar buyouts have dozens of billions of dollars of debt on their books. Thanks to the rough economy the revenue and profit projections that fund analysts have created for them are not going to pan out. Fund managers are certainly doing their best with the situation: They have taken advantage of the frothy debt markets to refinance their LBO debt so to lower their interest burdens. They are also trying to catch the stock market window and do their IPOs before it is too late. Yet the outlook remains somewhat poor. LPs look at debt-laden portfolio companies bought out at incredibly high prices and figure that it is better to get out now while there are still buyers in the market.

It is not common but since it does happen from time to time I thought it deserved a blurb. Lets you know that there is always an exception to everything.

***

It is all about the fees ...

Earlier in the book I spoke about the dire situation that pension funds all over the country are in. They have too few working people and employers putting money into their funds and too many retired workers taking money out of it. They need more money and fast.

I mentioned that one of the solutions that pension funds like Washington State Investment Board and CalPERS have found is to increase their portfolio allocation to "alternative investments", sending more and more money to the asset class. Private equity, being part of this asset class, has been a major beneficiary - collecting big management and incentive fees. Eventually though, they are going to have to own up to their clients, who have started to notice - and more importantly, grumble about - just how much these fees are costing them.

How prominent are these fees? Below is the schedule of fees for WSIB in 2010.

EQUITY SECURITIES:	Fees Paid
U.S. Active Equity Manager	$ 437,084
International Active Equity Managers	25,468,803
International Passive Equity Managers	1,688,645
U.S. Passive Equity Manager	999,273
Innovation Portfolio	2,814,849
ALTERNATIVE INVESTMENTS:	
Private Equity	144,862,277
Real Estate	23,018,937
Tangible Assets	704,747
CASH MANAGEMENT	851,560
OTHER FEES:	
Consultants and Advisors	557,904
Accounting	882,006
Legal Fees	162,188
Research Services	1,943,041
Miscellaneous Fees	70,133
Total Investment Expenses	$ 204,461,447

Courtesy of WSIB's 2010 Annual Report

WSIB paid $144.8 millions to outside firms to manage its private equity investments. The fees for investing and managing everything else - equities, real estate, and more - cost a mere $60 million. Recall earlier in the book that alternative investments compose 41% of the WSIB portfolio. So basically, 41% of WSIB's assets demand 71% of its investment fees.

Now to give credit where credit is due, private equity managers get these fees because private equity is hard and historically these assets have done better than just plain stocks and bonds. That being said, these pension funds are not going to sit around like crippled ducks taking fees at their face value. Pension funds today - especially core clients - hardly ever pay the sticker fee price, the "standard" 2 and 20. They are fierce negotiators at the table.

But not only that, these pension funds are pushing for more and more of the private equity spoils, as the next few sections will illustrate.

***

Co-investing. What is it and why do LPs like it?

It took me a while to understand what it meant to do a co-invest. Took just as long to figure out why people would care about it. While I was on the fund marketing side of the business the term often appeared in client inquiries. The fund managers I worked with gave very bland answers to each of these inquiries - which means that they would rather not hear the question turn up at all. While I worked in fund oversight research it was one of the first questions the firm asked prospective GPs. What on earth does it mean? As it turns out, **co-investing is a more of a granted privilege rather than a preordained right**. The GP's willingness to dole it out gives you a vague sense of how much they want you as an investor. There is a lot more to it than that, mind you, but broadly speaking you would not be wrong there.

Private equity's most important sources of capital are the large pension funds or sovereign wealth funds across the world. Though the gig has been lucrative for all parties involved, as time passed it became clear that the pension funds and their peers wanted to **get more involved in the deal making process**. Aware of their status as the **largest and most important source of investment capital for their clients**, they were quick to exercise that leverage to create better opportunities for themselves and the people who depend on them.

Let's say the pension fund for the penguins of Antarctica (Penguin Public Employee Retirement System, or PenPERS) contacts our favorite fictional PE firm, HTT & Co., with interest in investing in their latest PE fund, HTT Capital Appreciation III. The partners at the PE firm are naturally pleased as it means they have finally gotten the attention of the big boys (maybe the Macaws of Brazil would be interested in investing too!) but PenPERS did not get to its size by being a soft-belly. Soon as they sit down at the table, they politely mention to HTT that they find the terms of investing a little disagreeable for their taste. After all, they are stewards of public money and the public should deserve a very good deal. If HTT is not willing to provide this deal then PenPERS is perfectly okay with walking away.

HTT considers what they can offer. They bring up the possibility of a lower management fee. The PenPERS representative watches quietly. Anything else?

How about a lower incentive fee too? This is a juicy carrot. Again, the representative subtly angles for more.

The HTT partner is somewhat exasperated. Well then? With a gruff squawk, PenPERS makes it clear to HTT that they want co-invest rights. They want the opportunity to put their own money into a deal HTT might have in the pipeline.

It sounds at first redundant. If PenPERS is invested in a fund, aren't they already investing in HTT's deals? Yes, but a co-investor gets additional benefits that a normal LP investor would not get.

In a co-invest arrangement, a **limited partner gets preference in that they get to see a deal that is in the works and decide to put their money into the deal *alongside* the general partner**. A second smaller fund just for these co-investors is set up on the side of the main fund. There, PenPERS gets to make a direct investment in OpCo. The result is that essentially two entities, PenPERS and HTT, are making an investments in OpCo that is different than the normal situation where the investment comes from just one firm, HTT.

The end result is that PenPERS gets the opportunity to **double down on deals they especially favor** and also as a bonus **receives a very real economic boon called "not paying fees"**. Most often these co-invest funds do not charge a management fee, though they do sometimes charge the incentive fees. Most LPs are fine with that. They do not mind paying the GP money if they themselves are raking in the cash.

In the legal documents that establish a fund's existence, the GP gets a lot of power to decide which deals are open to a co-invest and which LP can do it. It is a powerful marketing tool but one that should be used sparingly. After all, the firm would like to get paid some management fees so to keep the doors open. Yet at the same time, a picky and prestigious LP can serve as an <u>anchor investor</u> - an investment that also serves as a big fat approval rating that you can shuck to the other institutions on your fund marketing list. Those other LPs, realizing that the anchor investor is likely going to look out for everyone's best interests, gets that much more interested in investing. Those guys, however, probably would not get the same privileges.

***

Why are some pension funds making private equity deals?

Earlier in this book, I discussed some of the reasons why institutional investors like private equity. I also briefly touched upon the subject of why pension funds did not do their own private equity deals. Let me review for a second here ...

First, a pension fund must look after up to $200 billion worth of pension assets and since alternative investments in theory make up only a small portion of the total portfolio it would make little sense for such an institution to spend an outsized portion of its time bothering with it.

Second, it is often believed that a mere pension fund would not be able to attract the same caliber of talent that a glamorous, high-powered private equity firm in a skyscraping suite could. A mere pension fund would not be able to offer the private equity pay or the private equity perks. As a steward of the public's money, they would find themselves open to strident criticism.

Third, hiring a private equity manager allows the pension fund to pin the shame of a bad investment on a very highly paid scapegoat.

These reasons, and along with them the traditional pension fund investment model, have begun to see recent cracks. It has become increasingly clear that alternative investments (which includes private equity) has grown to dominate the pension fund portfolio. Some pension funds are dedicating up to 40% of everything they have to hedge funds and private equity, a significant percentage. In addition, the fees being paid to private equity are coming to dominate pensions' total expenses, growing into the nine figure range.

And yes, it would probably take your boring pension fund years, a boatload of contacts, and a prestigious name to build a world-class private equity firm like KKR or TPG ... but several hundred million dollars and a sluggish job market in the finance sector can buy you a pretty damn good one. Lured by the potential of saving hundreds of millions, pension funds have been casting aside their managers and taking their investing in-house. Some have been taking baby steps in the process, doing co-invests and arranging very small side-deals on their own but one fund in particular has really gone all in on the idea.

Ontario Teachers' Pension Plan ("OTPP") is the third largest pension fund in Canada, but that is not what makes it unique. The $107.5 billion pension fund is more well known for owning and operating its own private equity investing arm, competing against other private equity firms for juicy, profit-making deals. Over the past 20 years, Ontario Teachers' has made over 200 direct investments in companies across the globe. And if for any reason you may think that because Ontario is a pension fund they are a cuter or cuddlier private equity fund, then you would be surprised to find that the suits working up north have elbows just as sharp as their Manhattan cohorts. Just Google "Ontario Teachers hostile takeover" and see. They are the epitome of the direct investing model.

***

The most obvious benefit is that running and operating your own private equity investing arm eliminates the need to pay outsized fees to outside private equity groups. Is it really so? Whether the benefit is all that much attractive considering the outside costs of building and maintaining accounts required for world-class private equity investing group is uncertain. If you want to attract world-class talent, you have to pay them world-class salaries. Considering how hard a bargain that these pension funds are already driving with their managers, the savings may not add up to all that much. So, this first "benefit" could be just a red herring.

One of the real benefits is the ability to control your own destiny and having complete knowledge of your portfolio. Because you are the one doing your own investing, you know what you're getting into and there is no secondary firm to get in between you and the investments. Investors want to know what's going on with our money and all too often alternative investment managers fail to provide that transparency. The more you know, the more you are able to plan for the future. Budgets can be forecasted and payments can be assured.

A real advantage that an in-house private equity arm has over traditional private equity firms is the source of capital. If you are a private equity firm you're constantly thinking about the exit strategy because your investors are standing on the sidelines tapping their feet and waiting for their returns. And even though these investors sign on to lock their money in for many years, it is very difficult to bring appreciable operating changes to accompany in just three or four years especially if those years are recession years. A pension fund can afford to be incredibly patient with its own capital. Part of this is because of the increased transparency, but it is also because the way pension accounting works liabilities can be deferred for many decades. A pension fund can be technically insolvent for years before the chickens really come home to roost. This gives the manager the time to wait out recessions, building real changes, and find the most optimal exit.

Despite how good it sounds, there are real risks to consider. First and foremost are the immense challenges associated with building a competent investing system outside of the traditional private equity ecosystem. For example, how much should the private equity employees be paid? The instinctive answer is: "not a whole lot". After all, the idea is to save yourself money, right? The problem there is that private equity employees know their own worth, and they will not come work for a pittance. And the ones who do end up on the job are likely to give it a halfhearted effort because they know that they are going to get paid no matter what their efforts yield. So you have to tie the employees' pay to their performance in a big way, and pay them in a big way if their work yields fruit. That might foster tensions with the rest of the company, which ultimately might end up creating a toxic workplace.

In addition, there are serious conflicts of interest that must be anticipated, openly discussed, and headed off at the pass. In recent years, there had been a spate of resignations triggered by unsightly behavior where decision-makers at pension funds would receive gifts from third-party agents hired by potential hedge fund clients and then end up picking those hedge funds for a big multimillion dollar investment. For a steward of the public purse, this violates the spirit of the law if not the law itself. Because an in-house private equity investing arm would be interacting with the great number of third parties, the potential for additional conflicts of interest grows ever more so and measures must be implemented to prevent them.

***

Despite the many risks and the hassle and turmoil of building an investing organization from scratch, many institutional investors have started to warm to the idea. In late 2010, South Carolina's pension fund announced that it would create an independent firm to oversee its private equity holdings, the first of its kind in the United States.[56] It is estimated that doing this would save South Carolina about $2 billion in fees and other associated costs over the next decade. CalPERS has followed suit, announcing that it directly invest up to a third of its $1.3 billion infrastructure portfolio - which includes things like bridges, roads, and other solid assets that generally do not include traditional real estate.

Now, if this sort of thing starts catching on then it would be a very troubling thing for the private equity industry. But those people are no sitting ducks, and have offered concessions to keep their valued clients. For example, many more co-investment opportunities. The idea here being that it is worth giving up those fees in order to maintain that business relationship where the pension funds rely on the private equity industry to source the best deals. It is all about long-term, right?

---

[56] The New York Times has a great overview here:
http://www.nytimes.com/2010/09/28/business/28carolina.html?_r=1&dbk

Another tactic is the recent prominence of managed accounts. These are private portfolios run by private equity managers for a favored client. One such deal was Texas Teachers' $3 billion managed account with KKR and Apollo Global Management.[57] Such arrangements are indicative of pension funds' increased leverage with their managers: a client with a managed account has a great deal more transparency into and say on what is happening with their invested money. Especially now with the financial crisis of 2008 slowing private equity fund raising, it is just getting harder and harder to find dollars to pump into those funds.

So the new challenges of private equity: Increased competition for good deals, a scarcity of debt for leveraged buyouts, and irritated LPs tightening the screws on how you run the business. What can I say? Private equity is a tough business.

---

[57] For another great article on this, read this: http://www.pionline.com/article/20111201/REG/111209997/

Private Equity Funds Owning Hedge Funds

Like one of those awesome matryoshka dolls

I have mentioned on two occasions that **certain large private equity firms have started hedge funds of their own as a side business**. Sounds intriguing right? Not trying to be coy. I swear that I was getting to it and now here we are.

Let me tell you a long story. The largest private equity firms were privately owned for a long time. Blackstone, Carlyle, KKR, and the like were partnerships owned by their partners and nobody else. The partners held all the shares. **But time and money eventually forced these companies to go public**. Why? A partnership is owned by its partners, who keep "capital accounts" in the partnership. This is kind of like to them what public stock is to you or me. Just as your shares of Microsoft stock represent the wealth you have that is "locked up" in Microsoft, the capital account represents the theoretical wealth the partners have "locked up" in the partnership. When a partner retires, he cashes out his partner capital account so that he can retire to Hawaii (or Tahiti or whatever). That cash out money is money that the partnership has to come up with somehow.

It eventually came to be the case that at these firms the oldest partners' capital accounts had grown to such an amount that if they did retire, the act of cashing out their account would pretty much ruin the whole company. The partners considered the risks: **They**

236

can go public or risk being ruined every time an old partner retired or died.
Going public means a steady source of capital from the public markets because the
company can sell its shares into the market. It means you can retain good employees by
giving them stock in the company. It means stability for a firm who has to provide top
level services for decades on end (since their investment horizons are so long).

These are all attractive perks so the private equity funds went public. But being a public
company brings with it a whole new set of baggage. Investors who buy and hold the
stock are going to be looking for growth. Growth in revenues or profits. Either one of
these bring growth in the stock. If the company cannot grow then the stock price
collapses and their employees' wealth evaporates.

The story is taking a while to grow. Stay with me! A private equity firm makes its
revenues from management fees (from managing its funds) and incentive fees (from its
successful deals). **The problem is that eventually the large-cap private equity
deals are going to dry up.** There are only so many attractive companies that can be
acquired. Only so many countries in the world with laws and shareholding cultures well-
developed enough to support a LBO culture. The private equity fund business is not
going to die anytime soon but it will not provide the growth that investors want. What
then?

**The answer for many firms was to extend the private equity brand into
hedge funds.** Firms like Blackstone and KKR have huge cachet in the finance world: A
wealth of contacts, huge deal flow, and deep operating experience/knowledge. The same
advantages that work with the private equity business overlap with the hedge fund

business as well. The business proposal that these firms brought to potential investors was this: We can bring the expertise we developed in PE investing to plain bond and stock investing too. Also, private equity firms can take on more risk than banks can. KKR hired some top traders from Goldman Sachs to run a long/short hedge fund. Goldman did not want to lose those guys but were forced to by the new bank regulations. Firm partners leveraged their institutional investor contacts to line up LPs for their hedge funds and raised a lot of money real fast. Things were good.

There are drawbacks. Managing a hedge fund is not as profitable as managing a private equity fund. The management fee percentage is the same 2% but the incentive fee revenue is smaller. So far the investors have not minded this because for the most part the burgeoning hedge fund business has delivered on its growth promises. It seems to be an easy way to find some extra revenue for the firm. I have heard of a few other smaller private equity funds starting their own hedge businesses on the side.

So the fee issue is not a big one but this next one though is. It is about the information and investing conflicts you are going to get when a private equity fund owns a hedge fund. Let us talk about them and they are very subtle so do not worry if you do not get it immediately. **For one thing, a hedge fund invests in public securities**. They buy public stock or bonds and so they are only allowed to use public information to make those decisions. **Yet on another branch of the company are the private equity people, who regularly get access to information that is not public**. The PE people have to be very careful to keep this knowledge in-house. The hedge fund staff working on the other side of the building should not know about this information and they should definitely not trade on it. Otherwise it can amount to insider trading and a very nice phone call from the SEC. Yet ... the marketing text that you are sending to your potential LPs says that you can **cross-pollinate expertise from the PE side to the public side**. In fact, one of the biggest reasons you think you have an advantage over the other hedge funds is the fact that you have this private equity expertise that you can draw on. How is that going to work out?

One place I worked at had this issue and the solution they came up with was to build a very strict "Chinese Wall" between the publics and the privates. The public people work in a separate location from the private people. If any people with private information do visit this office then they stay in an empty wing of the building separated from everyone else by a physical glass wall. They did not encourage much conversation - even daily chit-chat - as well. And if something does happen and information is accidentally leaked then "procedures" are put into place to remove any potential issues. I was never in a position to find out what those are and probably did not want to know either.

Another conflict - very artfully pointed out by an astute institutional investor - involves the investments that these funds make. It is not uncommon to see a hedge fund investing in debt from a leveraged buyout executed by its associated "parent" private equity fund. Such things happen because the personnel share similar convictions on their investment strategies. It does however bring up concerns. To let you know why this matters, let me go back to the HTT example. Let us say HTT bought OpCo and issued a lot of junk bonds to do it. HTT runs a hedge fund business on the side and the manager running that fund, working on a similar investment thesis, buy the junk bonds for their own investors.

So far so good but **what happens if OpCo is not a good investment and starts to wobble and fail**? The debt from the leveraged buyout is too much and if the company has to keep paying the stone-heavy interest payments then it is going to go bankrupt. Management has to reduce the debt load somehow and to get such an arrangement they go to the debt's owners ... which include an HTT fund manager.

The situation is now a mess. HTT's hedge fund investors are not the same as HTT's private equity fund investors. Both investors are going to have to take a hit on this bad investment. That is unavoidable. Yet who gets the brunt of it? In theory the equity-holders should. After all, they take the most risk along with the most reward. A person who owns stock only gets paid in bankruptcy court after all the bond holders get paid. Yet the hedge fund owning the debt is a direct subsidiary of the private equity firm. **It seems likely that pressure could come down on the hedge fund side to agree to a deal that saves the equity holders at some cost to the bond holders.** How can the firm equitably resolve this conflict?

More importantly, how can they let their investors know that the conflict is to be resolved equitably? An investor is already going to be suspicious by the fact that the hedge fund is investing in its parent's deals. If HTT bought OpCo in an LBO and HTT's hedge fund bought OpCo's LBO debt, a concerned investor can say with reason that the hedge fund was forced to "soak up" the LBO's junk bond debt so those bonds can have a market. **Now that the company is in trouble and that debt might not get paid**

back, investors might feel that the hedge fund manager is going to look out for the best interests of his employer rather than that of the investors in his own fund.

In response to this, big firms have started conflict boards staffed with independent arbitrators to work through the problem. Usually the existence of such a board along with some strict rules of engagement are enough for the due diligence process. Someone can go and check the box on that one. Probably the biggest thing they are banking on though really is that the investment stays out of rocky straits. A conflict like the kind I thought up can leave a lot of bruises on both sides.

Private equity firms are always going to do what they did before. You cannot teach an old dog new tricks after all. They grind for private equity deals, run their investments, exit the investment at a gain, and then do it again. That is what they do the best. But the industry is over a quarter of a century old and like as with any other mature industry the players cannot keep digging up the same corner day after day. Things have to change with all the good and bad that comes with it.

Outside America

What is the state of private equity outside of the US?

It has always been hard to find a good deal, but as the marketplace globalizes the rat race gets only more frantic. With the advent of resource nationalism and a beginning of trends like RMB-denominated funds, private equity groups have to change their styles and get comfortable with different ways to run an investment.

The LBO is a rare beast, and people give it a lot of attention because it happens in the US and it is a huge event. Precisely because it is a huge event that upends management and transfers companies' ownership, it rarely happens outside of the US. Some have closed a few buyouts in Europe but in general they are rare outside of the States. **The regulations are tougher, the financing is harder to come by, and a lot of the time, the cultural differences are such that it makes a complete buyout almost impossible.** Big companies are run by families and a PE firm is not interested in being a carrier of the dynastic crown. The US is a good place for LBOs because control more often lies with investors rather than a founding family, the financial markets are large enough so that an IPO is possible, and the law allows an LBO to happen at all.

But that does not mean that PE groups do not exist outside of the US. Many do and some operate almost exclusively overseas,[58] competing for deals alongside overseas

---

[58] I once attended a presentation by an African private equity group, investing money in building private

branches of the large established US-based firms. But these smaller firms do not take entire companies private. Most of the time they work with and take equity stakes in the companies. The company needs money and the investor has money. As a result, the PE group gets a stake (usually in the form of some sort of financial security that offers more protection than common equity yet has more upside than a bond, a hybrid instrument like a preferred security or a convertible bond)[59] and the family gets money with which to expand the business. These types of private equity deals, which are a mainstay of the smaller private equity fund community, happen a lot in China, Indonesia, and other developing markets.

It makes good sense to let the family run the business anyway, because they know how to pull the levers in an often alien culture where the rule of law (as well as the separation between the state and its commerce) is not as strong and the code of conduct as well as the economics of the industry are utterly cryptic and hieroglyphic to any foreigner. **One only needs to hear the horror stories of private investment groups who got their pants handed back to them in tempting but challenging countries like Russia and China.** If a PE group crosses the wrong person, then they can find themselves visited by mysterious "government checks" or afflicted by unique "regulations." If you are an investor you cannot really do anything about it, because the

---

hospitals for villagers in sub-Saharan Africa. They run an interesting business, because there are no public markets to which one can exit an investment. They literally must run it until the money is recouped. Fascinating work, really. They must really get the "exit strategy" question a lot because they addressed it first in their presentation.

[59] In case it slipped your mind, a preferred security is more "protected" than a normal share of common stock. It receives dividends but does not allow the holder to vote on any of the company's actions like a common stock shareholder would. A convertible bond is a bond that turns into normal equity shares. Another frequently used security in this line of work are bonds with detachable warrants, allowing the holder to purchase stock at an agreed upon price (sort of like options, but in this case they are issued by the company).

243

courts in those countries are not quite the same as those in the US, and let's leave it at that. You can wave a contract around in China as much as you want, but **over there, it is just a piece of paper**.

As I mentioned earlier, there are great risks in investing in foreign markets. Nothing is the same - the culture, competition or the laws. Though it may be true that in the past foreign governments welcomed foreign investment, hoping to benefit from the development opportunities it brings, that attitude tends to change as time passes. Native citizens are not fond of watching foreign money flood their markets and they are especially not happy to see the fruits of their hard work - all the money that they worked for - head back out of the country so that rich American fat cats can get fatter than they already are.

In addition, due to the nuances of money flooding in and out of a country, there are negative economic effects to having everyone trying to get their foot in the door. Such effects include rampant inflation and a weaker export sector (due to a stronger currency). To avoid them, **government officials might take steps to curtail the outsiders and preserve the fruits of their citizens' labor**. This is good for the citizens, but terrible for private equity funds left on the outside looking in.

A Chinese Private Equity Story

Once upon a time in China ...

I want to tell a Chinese private equity story. Early on, Chinese private equity funds were exploding like no other fund of their type. They were batting a thousand from the leadoff spot to the nine hole. China's economy grew fast but all the companies operating in them were mega-sized state-owned companies and tiny mom-and-pop shops. **A middle class of leading billion dollar businesses had yet to emerge**. This meant that a savvy investor with the right number of contacts could get in on a future Nike or Johnson & Johnson at the ground floor just as it starts to hit its stride. Once the company went public, the investor made many times their money. Like shooting fish in a barrel.

The earliest private equity funds were created in the late 1990s as joint ventures between investment banks like Goldman Sachs and domestic Chinese companies. Then those teams spun out on their own, starting private equity firms to pull investors from their money and scour the country for good deals.

They all made **obscene** returns. If a fund makes returns of 20% to 25% a year investing in the United States and Europe, its marketing group is going to crow that to the hills and beyond. And they should because for the US, a mature market, 20-25% is great. It takes a lot of effort and work to get those results, balancing top notch operating experience with a judicious use of leverage. **People used to seeing American performance numbers often spew their coffee reviewing Chinese private**

equity. A fund that makes 20-25% a year in China is something of a laggard. Top notch funds with the right connections and operating experience regularly made 40-50% returns on their entire funds *without leverage.* If a portfolio company did not grow its revenues by 30% from one year to the next, then that was cause for concern.

Thanks to the size, growth, and infrastructure of the Chinese economy, a company can double revenues in just a single year. That is a 100% growth. Then the next year the company grows another 75% just to make sure you were paying attention. Most amazingly, the returns hardly felt the effects of the law of declining returns. The funds got larger, but the returns still dropped your jaws. Private equity at its best. These funds invested and harvested through the 2008 financial crisis and still came out smelling roses. **No hedge fund manager can make 40-50% returns year after year for half a decade through some of the toughest investing years in world history.** Performance that fulfills private equity's potential.

Here is a very nice looking chart from Preqin Ltd, which is one of the most commonly accessed private equity-related data sources. It displays the top 10 Asia-Pacific private equity funds by performance. This performance is represented by a metric called net IRR. IRR stands for internal rate of return net of fees, and it is a mathematical calculation that says, "Hey each year your fund investment grew by this so and so amount percentage."

Rank	Fund	Firm	Vintage	Fund Size (mn)	Type	Net IRR (%)
1	AMWIN Innovation Fund	CHAMP Ventures	1998	42 AUD	Early Stage	1,025.1
2	Development Partners Fund	Development Principles Group	2005	81 USD	Growth	105.5
3	Vietnam Equity Fund	Finansa Fund Management	2005	15 USD	Expansion / Late Stage	104.9
4	Headland Asian Ventures Fund 3	Headland Capital Partners	2008	230 USD	Venture	94.7
5	BankInvest Private Equity New Markets II	BankInvest	2008	100 USD	Growth	71.1
6	Baring Asia Private Equity Fund III	Baring Private Equity Asia	2005	490 USD	Balanced	66.2
7	USIT I	JAFCO (Japan)	1994	7,000 JPY	Venture	63.8
8	USIT II	JAFCO (Japan)	1997	10,300 JPY	Venture	63.7
9	Ant Bridge No.1	Ant Capital Partners	2003	2,500 JPY	Direct Secondaries	59.2
10	Pacific Equity Partners Supplementary Fund II	Pacific Equity Partners	2004	162 AUD	Buyout	59.0

If the graphic is not easily visible to you, the top performing fund was raised in Australia: A 42 million AUD fund started in 1998 called AMWIN Innovation Fund. Its net IRR was 1,025%. This means that every year, your investment in AMWIN went up 1,025%. Or ten times. Think about that. It is not just a case of "the early bird gets the worm" too. The 3rd and 4th best performing funds were raised in 2008, and returned 94.7% and 71.1% net IRR. And bigger here also meant better: Those two funds were both over $100 million large.

(Even more amazing to consider is that these returns are net of fees. If a private equity fund manager took the normal fee cut of 2 and 20, then the actual returns were even higher!)

Considering the wild successes, it is understandable that soon everyone wanted a Chinese private equity fund of their own. This led to several problems. For one thing, these early Chinese funds took advantage of a variety of complex laws, loopholes, and offshore trusts to get around restrictions designed to prevent foreigners from owning stakes in certain Chinese companies and property. Secondly, all the economic issues that I talked about earlier started to appear in the overheating economy. This started to alarm government officials who feared that these foreign-born issues together with other homegrown ones would sink the Chinese economic miracle (and more importantly throw them out of power).

One new thing they tried was enabling competitor funds called RMB denominated funds (RMB being the Chinese yuan). American and European investors with their dollars and euro can only invest in the dollar funds, not these unique RMB funds. Then they mandated that **dollar funds cannot invest in certain sectors**. Only the RMB funds can, a fantastic edge for domestic investors and a real problem for the foreigners. It quickly established a dual class system. **One fund is for the foreigners and the better one is for the natives.** Even large American private equity funds with experience in China like the Carlyle Group have begun to raise RMB denominated funds of their own. However, they can often only do so in partnerships with domestic bodies. And of course, the RMB designation means that their usual preferred LPs back home are left outside looking in. They have to build a Chinese investor base from scratch.

Such resource "nationalism" - this interest to keep profits in-house - continues to manifest itself in other growing countries like Brazil, **who mulls over a tax on foreign investment**. The sentiment is definitely understandable - Americans hardly welcome foreign investors with open arms - but losing the growth can sting.

Another Chinese Private Equity Story

Once upon a time in China Part II ...

Want to hear another Chinese private equity story? This one is about how much of a difference country and culture can make in private equity investing. In China, there is a tier of firms with a long track record of excellent performance. Some have been working in private equity since the late 90's, right at the very birth of the industry. Their networks are deep, entrepreneurs trust their capabilities, and they know how to take a company from zero to sixty to IPO. The decade old track record speaks for itself. Any investor would appreciate their services.

Then there are other firms who do not have the same record but sport what the Chinese called "*guanxi*", which roughly translated means "connections". One in particular, New Horizon Capital, is quite fascinating. You have two co-founders running the place. One co-founder is an excellent investor with the right experience and Ivy League credentials. He is undoubtedly impressive, but there is nothing really all that special about that pedigree. There are schools of big Ivy League tuna swimming around the private equity ocean.

No, the intriguing thing is New Horizon's other co-founder, Wen Yunsong, better known as the son of Chinese premier Wen Jiabao, the once-third-highest ranked Chinese politician in the country and the one in charge of the entire economy. **Being the offspring of a highly ranked politician never failed to hurt your chances at wealth but in a country like China, where the government holds the most**

power, it is a one-of-a-kind edge. Businesspeople give you perks and send through all their best deal flow. Entrepreneurs are immediately primed to do business with you. Regulatory approvals for deals get done faster and the officials give you the benefit of the doubt. Investors will salivate at the possibilities. It is hard to even begin imagining them!

The funny thing is that its special guanxi is sort of an **open secret**. Mr. Wen's heritage is not mentioned at all in any of the pitchbooks or the fund's other marketing material. Their competitors, including many in the first tier, acknowledge it with a wink and a nod but do not want to say anything more about it. **If you were an investment advisor, would you tell your clients about this secret?** It is not like the Chinese really want you blabbing to people that the kids of their top government officials are starting private equity funds and making millions of dollars. At the same time, if nobody said anything then New Horizon would be a tough sell. Outside of Mr. Wen there is **absolutely nothing particularly special** about this one firm. Its track record is nowhere as long or great and its other personnel are nothing to write home about. Your clients are going to either think that you are an idiot or suspect something is up and fire you anyway.

(In the end, this type of information should probably be divulged to the clients. They are the ones paying you after all, and the trust between you and the fund would be a small price to pay for maintaining the trust between you and your client. Nothing stays a secret forever anyway. I just Googled New Horizon and found a multitude of articles identifying its special sauce.)

Fascinating story springing from the cultural differences between China and the United States. In China, offspring like those of Mr. Wen - called "princelings" - attract some real money as fund managers. You do not find this so much the case in the United States. Chelsea Clinton worked for a hedge fund but that hire does not help make returns. **Starting a private equity fund around some Kennedys would probably get you nowhere.** China's government and family culture is such that being a princeling can make all the difference. Goes to show you how alien the one country is from the next. Private equity funds expanding from the US into the foreign diaspora should know that doing it the same way they always did is not going to work as it always did.

Venture Capital

What is venture capital about?

I live in San Francisco and venture capital is a huge player in the area, focusing on the technology companies so prevalent in the Bay Area. Their money and the companies that it backs adds a lot to the economy here. The name has a lot of cachet here. What do they do? Why are they special?

Venture capital is more of a marketing term than anything. In substance what they do is similar to that of a private equity group except that they are smaller, do not do buyouts, and invest in things with incredibly high risk profiles. An investment is more likely to collapse in a steaming pile of failure than bust out big like a Google or an Apple.

Like the foreign private equity groups I wrote about earlier, **they do not do leveraged buyouts**. If they claim to do so then they are a venture capital firm. This is partly because of the tiny size of their investments and partly because of their enormous risk profile. It would be insane to lever up on such a bet. Instead, these funds take stakes through specially constructed securities. Often these are hybrid stock-bond financial instruments such as preferred stock or convertible bonds. Their hybrid nature gives the potential for upside while protecting invested capital in case stuff does go south.

Beyond financial capital, the **venture capitalist also provides strategic guidance, contacts, and operating experience that the founders would not often otherwise be able to obtain**. Google famously hired Eric Schmidt for its CEO because the venture capitalists insisted on such. Schmidt then guided the company to a multi-billion dollar IPO and an explosive rise into Silicon Valley royalty. Vinod Khosla made billions from a tiny investment in Juniper Networks, but played a large role in the company's development. His investment would not have panned out as well had he not been so involved.

It so makes a lot of sense then that some of the best venture capitalists have been successful as entrepreneurs. Khosla was one of the founders of Sun Microsystems and grew it into a leader in the industry. Andreessen Horowitz is a successful venture capital firm that bought and later sold Skype. Founder Marc Andreessen had founded Netscape, the dominant web browser before Bill Gates decided otherwise. If you want to get hired by a venture capital firm for technology, then you probably should first start a company and take it big. Easier said than done, of course.

Venture capital is such a deep topic that it deserves its own book. This chapter would not be enough to do the whole thing justice. Instead, for the next few pages I would like to discuss certain rising trends that I have noticed in the space, centered on a core thesis that I do not think would be very hard to miss. Let's start with the secondary exchanges.

***

Of Interest: Corporate Venture Capital

In the "Creating Value at OpCo" sub-section of this book, I mentioned "strategic buyers". These are companies who are interested in a PE firm's investment because they think purchasing the company would help their overall business prospects. The key thing to note here is that a strategic buyer's core business is not investment - it is to sell a product to its customers. Thus, why the phrase "strategic" is part of the term. It is a portion of their overall business strategy. Keep this in mind as I now introduce "strategic venture capital", which has been a rising trend for many companies.

A strategic venture capital fund is set up by an established company to invest in smaller startups. It is often arranged as a separate subsidiary and may have its own offices and dedicated employees. However, its end-goal mission is very much aligned with its parent: Make good investments and help the parent company succeed.

Probably the most prominent example of Corporate Venture Capital is Intel Capital, which is the venture capital investing arm for the massive chip-maker. Set up in 1991, Intel Capital is today one of the largest technology venture capital firms in the world, creating themed funds that invest in wireless networking, chip technologies, and the like. They have invested over ten billion dollars across a thousand plus companies all over the world. Other companies have attempted to replicate this success. Google Ventures, for example, is a very well-known venture capital fund that has gained a whole lot of prominence in recent years. Even non-tech companies get in on the action. In July 2010 General Motors - the car maker - set up General Motors Ventures, looking to make investments in technology companies creating exciting products that GM might eventually be interested in. And LVMH - owner of Louis Vuitton - runs a private equity arm of its own called L Capital Asia, which manages over a $1 billion to invest in companies that can and will become valuable retailing partners to the parent company.

These investing organizations - Google Ventures, General Motors Ventures, and Intel Capital - were created for reasons beyond simple profit maximization. In other words, these are not initiatives set up by the parent companies because they have some extra cash lying around and wanted to make the best of it (and if they wanted to see the best returns for their cash then investing it in VC would be a poor choice as we will discuss in the next chapter). There are powerful strategic benefits of having these VC and private equity arms. Their investing subsidiaries serve as the "eyes and ears" of their organization, alerting their higher-ups to potential acquisitions, partners, and most importantly, competitors.

I want to drill deeper into what I mean when I say "competitor". For startups offering some novel service or product, there is one crucial question that all investors are going to ask: What's the market for that? That is a tough question to answer because it requires a deep understanding of the overall industry, one's own product, and how badly customers would want it. More often than not, it is a subjective "art" on par with fortune telling and water dowsing - might as well throw a stick into the air and go in the direction where it points. What many have done is not to go to Excel and construct a big sprawling spreadsheet but instead to point to a large, publicly traded company and say, "We want to go after their market and their revenues. We want to take their customers away from them." Investors get the point very quickly.

This is a great tactic for a startup: It helps focus the startup's employees on what matters and gets the point across to investors about what is exciting about their new product. It is not so hot for the publicly traded companies that the startups are gunning after. Too many times, head management at incumbent players have dismissed small upstarts as misfit trends for misfit customers, only to find their businesses (and jobs) trampled by these "misfit trends". Intel's worst nightmare is the company missing some broad technological trend that leaves them by the wayside. Intel Capital's job is to make sure that does not happen, keeping tabs on tech happenings around the world.

Creating a dedicated venture capital fund is one of the best ways to encourage and grow an "ecosystem" around a company's product. The goal is to get other, smaller companies lashed to your own company's product, creating a competitive moat between yourself and your competitors. Going back to our Intel Capital example, the "ecosystem" revolves around Intel's chip business and the demand for processor speed: What Intel Capital hopes to encourage with its investments is the growth of companies whose products would require consumers to buy faster and faster computers, fueling demand for Intel's chips. So having an in-house venture capital arm is worth for a lot more than just an expensive alarm system - it can very well enhance the company's strengths and protect its revenue generators.

So those are the benefits of having an in-house venture fund. Here are the drawbacks: It is hard. Things will fail. It must be allowed to fail from time to time. Like all successful subsidiary projects, a corporate venture capital fund has to have its independence or it cannot succeed. There will be failed investments and lost money - that is just the nature of the beast - and the parent company should know what it is getting into.

**

Venture Capital Returns

So I have been dancing around it up until now but I think now I am going to come out and say it: Venture capital investing is hard. Very few companies do it well and the returns show it. Even though the private secondary markets make it much easier to return money to the LPs in a reasonable amount of time, the fact is that since the dotcom bust the majority of venture capital funds have had middling returns. Take a look at the chart below, which charts the industry's total returns over the years. It might seem at first a little intimidating but we will walk through it together so that we can get a better sense of what this means.

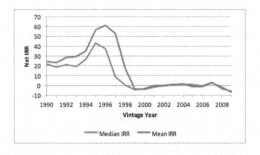

Credit: Cambridge Associates[60]

---

[60] You can find the data points behind this report here:

The two most confusing aspects of this chart are the terms "**IRR**" and "**Vintage Year**". Let me explain to you what some of these terms mean. IRR is an acronym that stands for "internal rate of return" and it is the standard metric[61] to judge the performance of an investment whether it be a piece of real estate, a share in Apple, or money stashed in a venture capital fund. The higher the IRR is, the better of an economic opportunity it is. If all things were equal (by that I mean the stuff that cannot be measured in dollars and cents like environmental impact or long-tail catastrophe risk) then you want to be invested in things that give you a very high IRR. The vintage year corresponds to the year that the venture capital firm raised the fund. So a fund vintage 1999 was raised in the year 1999.

So to interpret: From the start of the chart in 1990 to about 1999, the returns were very good at some 15% to 20%. The mean - or average - IRR was much greater than the median IRR - the returns garnered by the firms at the exact numerical middle of the pack. This means that the top VC funds had very high returns to boost up the average. It supports the notion that in many investment circles there are the top-tier firms and then there is everyone else. The best firms are the best because they actually do outperform their competition. However, all these numbers - median and mean both - are distorted

http://www.nvca.org/index.php?option=com_content&view=article&id=78&Itemid=102

[61] The Wikipedia is a little sparse and chock full of finance terms but you can try it if you wish:

http://en.wikipedia.org/wiki/Internal_rate_of_return

by the huge success of the dotcom boom years. Now that those are starting to fall out of range, potential LPs find things to be concerned about. **Many venture capital funds offer middling returns that just barely manage to beat the public market after the boom boom years.[62] In fact, many of these funds (in some cases up to nearly a half - as according to the report by the Kauffman Foundation) lose money for their investors. Since 1999, both the median and mean IRR has been around 0%. Investors are better off if they invested in the SP500, NFL franchises, or even Treasury bills. In 2012, peHUB leaked a number of performance metrics from some of Sequoia Capital's funds dated 2010[63].** Three funds raised in 1999 and 2000 returned in a range of 3% to 11%. Not bad considering that the average venture capital fund raised in that period had negative IRR losses but a far cry from some of Sequoia's older funds like the 1998 Sequoia Capital VIII, which had an IRR Of 117%! But those days are seemingly gone, perhaps for good.

If you look at the returns that the investors actually get - that is, returns after fees and expenses - then it is all the more worse. This is pretty egregious because many of these venture capital funds have the same 2 and 20 fee and expense structure that many

---

[62] There is a great report by the Kauffman Foundation that looks at venture capital returns and I did a lot of reading here to find some of the quantitive data points.

You can find the document here: http://www.kauffman.org/newsroom/venture-capital-industry-must-shrink-to-be-an-economic-force-kauffman-foundation-study-finds.aspx

[63] You can read more here.

http://www.reuters.com/assets/print?aid=USL1E8H4ECM20120604

hedge funds and private equity funds have. The difference is that those funds have been seeing intense pressures from their investors to cut those fees down. There pressures do not exist with venture capital firms. Limited partners want to stay in good standing with their GPs so that they can get access to the next big fund so as a result they stay very hands off in regards to fund management. As it turns out, it seems like for everyone's sake (especially if it is a pension fund ... that's YOUR money being frittered away there!) they should be a little more harsh.

It gets worse. So, VC funds often do not return more money than they take in and they charge preposterous fees. What else? As it turns out, they hold their investors' money for way too long. Have you ever put money into a bank CD? You would not be able to touch your money for a long time but in return, there's some small amount more of it when that time has passed. A hedge fund is kind of like that but a venture capital fund much more so. With venture capital, you might not be able to see a return for years on end. After all, the venture capitalists have to wait until their investments grow up and are ready to sell for a nice fat payout and that wait can be for a very long time. Think of Facebook and how long it stayed private from its founding in 2004 to its IPO in 2012. These companies can stay private for a very long time and even if you can show the LPs the accounting records saying you have this huge paper gain ("Look at all this money we've made that you can't have yet!"), they want the cash back in their hands.

So the question is: If you are an investor and you know this kind of information, why on earth would you ever invest in a venture capital fund? **The idea behind venture capital investing - the idea that makes it worth - is that you take on a whole**

lot of risk because there is the possibility that you can see a whole lot more gain from it. There is a "risk premium" over the "market" as a whole (remember, the market being the return from holding EVERYTHING that you can possibly invest in within the whole entire world). But you are not getting that premium.

So yeah, that is not good for venture capital investing.

***

Startups and Venture Capital Today

In the previous chapter, you learned that despite big IPOs by Facebook, Twitter, and other private tech companies, venture capital funds struggle to deliver good returns. To learn more about why this effect is taking place, let's take a look at the startup world today and how those very startups themselves are changing and adapting in ways that make venture investing that much harder.

First, startups do not need that much money anymore. Thanks to new infrastructure offered by Amazon and Google, a company can get up and going without needing to spend very much. For example, my friend wants to start a web business. He knows a code language called Ruby-on-Rails and is a very good coder. **With a five dollar domain name, infrastructure space rented from Amazon for 9.5 cents an hour, and a few restless nights of coding, a company can run for less than a thousand dollars a year.** Why would they want to take on a million or so dollars from a VC firm and dilute their own stake?

Then the competition. In recent years a whole new class of investors have emerged to provide money to budding entrepreneurs. Among the first were angel investors. They are wealthy entrepreneurs who risk small lots of cash on budding companies. Sometimes they are investing in nothing more than an engineer duo and an idea. Angel investors do not put a lot of money into their ideas but it costs a lot less to run a startup business today. **They are independently wealthy and some do it less for the financial return than the thrill and excitement of being involved on the cutting edge of technology.** This is a good sentiment for them to have because the investments they take on are astoundingly risky, literally science experiments with no immediate commercial application. They manage this risk is by expanding the portfolio and taking on dozens of investments. It only adds to the intense competition already present in the industry.

Rising along with the angel investors are the business incubators, which gather small companies together into a single complex and seed them with connections, mentoring, office space and a small amount of money. **Y Combinator is the leading practitioner of the concept and has debuted quite a few successful startups such as Dropbox and AirBnB.** While the size of the investment is negligible, the connections and the mentoring is more than enough to make incubators like YC (as it is called) a hot destination. This dispersion of information within the YC community essentially turns the tables on traditional VC firms like Sequoia and Kleiner Perkins, who soon find that they are going to have to compete with one another to make investments in incubator companies. YC is thus at its heart a union for startups - leveraging its cachet to maximize the benefits of its member companies. Great for startups, but bad for venture capitalists, who are no longer the gate guardians of power in Silicon Valley.

Now let's talk about Kickstarter. Kickstarter (kickstarter.com) lets people go online and browse a large collection of project "proposals" from people with ideas. If someone likes an idea, they can make a "pledge" to that project and help it reach a monetary goal in return for some token gift (the way it goes, the more you pledge, the more impressive the gift becomes). Kickstarter has funded many projects that otherwise would not be able to attract funding from traditional venture capital sources. For example, as of mid-2012, the Kickstarter project that has attracted the most funding is Pebble, a cool e-paper watch that connects through Bluetooth to your iPhone. The project at first started out looking for $100,000 but ended up attracting over $9.5 million from over 63,000 people.[64]

---

[64] You can go check out the Kickstarter page for this product here:
http://www.kickstarter.com/projects/597507018/pebble-e-paper-watch-for-iphone-and-android

Looks pretty cool to me.

The Pebble

Now, people who have a cool idea do not have to give up stock and profits to another company. They can go onto Kickstarter, get people to like their ideas, and then get the funding to go do it!

Now, venture capital investing has always been a high wire act. Startups have a high miss rate and a manager would be glad if just one or two out of over a dozen picks do well. These new advancements in the field make it even harder for them going forward. There is more money sloshing around than ever before, the best companies need less money than ever before while having more avenues than ever to get it. **Yet if you look at it from the perspective of a consumer or an entrepreneur, these new developments are great!** Starting a company used to be a process that took a lot of money to get off the ground, which meant you had to have good connections with rich folks to even think about it. Starting up a company is today a much more democratic process.

These new changes mean more potentially life-bettering ideas can see light. It helps consumers because it gives them the chance to try out new products that would not be possible years ago. I use a product called Dropbox, which is an alumnus of the aforementioned Y Combinator. The program puts a folder on your desktop that is always synced to a server somewhere. Thus you can always access your files online. Brilliant concept. I have not carried a USB jump drive around in months because all my stuff is on Dropbox. Cannot imagine life without it, and if these progressions have not come about then I would have had to do so.

So it is not always about the returns.

Learning More ...

Cus this stuff is just so fascinating, am I right??

So here we come at the end of the discussion material. Now before I break out of instructor mode in the next section, I want to leave you with some additional reading material. If after coming to the end of this book you are still interested in learning more about the alternative investment industry, I am now comfortable enough to point you to some fairly intermediate and advanced economic material. They are mentioned here (and listed in no particular order or preference) because I have at one time found them to deliver useful and interesting insight.

So here goes nothing. I don't have URLs on here because they mess up the formatting but if you were to put these into Google you'll find the links right away. Bookmark them!

~ **Pension and Investments** - This niche website is always giving me fascinating tidbits about the sometimes tense relationship between alternative investment funds and their big clients. Not to mention their knack for digging up interesting data points.

~ **FT Alphaville** - The Financial Times has the best analysis on the global markets anywhere. The problem is that they have a pay wall that is as wide as the Congo River.

You can only get, like, one article a month and if you just happen to click on an uninteresting one then it sucks because you have to wait for another month before you can read again. Introducing FT Alphaville. It is a blog run by the Financial Times staff and thank God it is free to read all day and every day. This stuff can get very thick with jargon but if you stick to it I guarantee it will be worth your while.

~ **Dealbook** - Likewise with Dealbook, which is run by the New York Times. While the Grey Lady has a slightly less torturous paywall, it again does not apply to blogs. Dealbook, for all of its great material, is considered a blog. I certainly hope that remains the case. While all the articles are worth your time, I especially recommend anything written by Steven M. Davidoff, the Deal Professor. A former corporate lawyer, he writes some awe inspiring stuff on private equity.

~ **Fooling Some of the People All of the Time, a Long Short Story** - Written by David Einhorn, this book is one of the best things I have ever read. It is knee deep in the finance and accounting stuff so I would not recommend it to a beginner. If you can stick with it though, it is worth your while because Einhorn bares everything. You learn about his previous investments, his investing style, and the sheer research depth it takes to beat the market. Truly great stuff.

A Postscript's Introduction

So here I have come to the end of my little soapbox. I hope you enjoyed reading it. This is the first book I wrote since that time in high school when I conjured up a young adult novel about a human-vampire romance novel (guess I was ahead of my time). Every page was a struggle. I would write something, erase it, rewrite it with a dozen prefaces to make the definition work out just right, and then realize that nobody would understand what I meant with all those prefaces so I start over again.

In this book's introduction, I promised you two things: The best career advice I ever gave and a brief moral lesson.

The career advice comes in the form of four "work commandments" that I found to have always worked in any job I have been in. Mind you that I have not worked as a rough blue collar worker (like a truck driver) nor have I worked in one of those special-skill type jobs (like an engineer or a computer programmer). I only know what works for what I have gone through - white-collar "analyst" type jobs. Maybe my work commandments succeed in the blue collar and engineering jobs too. You would have find out on your own.

The moral lesson comes - fittingly for a finance-head like me - in the form of two numbers. A pair of numbers to keep in mind as you go about the future of your career. You can pull whatever other conclusions you wish from my explanation.

Here we go.

The Most Excellent Career-Development Advice I Ever Gave

I like to talk to people younger than I am. It makes me feel younger. And I also love to teach. Had it not been for the terrible economy and our society's unusual disdain for teachers, I would have ended up a high school algebra teacher and been perfectly satisfied doing so.

Whenever I was asked for any career development advice I would give them the standard stuff. Things like "Do what you want to do" and "Work hard". Then I realized that these tips are practically useless. They are blank platitudes that do not help people get to where they want to go and who they want to be.

I think people today want very practical tips. Seemingly foolish things that they can go out and do right now like **"Add some color to your resume with a tasteful dark blue line at the top"** or **"Lock yourself into a closet and talk into the dark right before a big presentation"**. They are not inspirational - probably would not sound so great in a graduation keynote - but they help people get to where they want. That's the point.

I have distilled all the lame practical tips I have given in my life into a four pointed list (in addition to the two that I have given above). Here goes nothing.

1) Google everything. There is a fun thing I like to do with some of my friends when they ask me lame questions. I send them a link that takes them to a website called "Let Me Google That For You". When you click on my link, a little flash animation plays that

270

shows a cursor clicking on the Google search box, typing in their simple question, and then asking "There! Was that so hard?" It is alternatively hilarious and obnoxious yet it is great advice. One day I wanted a new layout for my resume. I Googled "unique resume layouts". Wanted great interview questions for a job. Googled the company, Googled the industry and Googled for questions. **Google works.** Odds are that somebody out there has already asked and answered your question. Google skills that you hone on your own serve you well in the work space when you have to do "market research".

2) Make your cover letters short. Basically a cover letter is the introduction stage for your resume. It is the first thing that people see when they get your job application. I recommend that you write one universal cover letter and tweak it for every job that comes along. **Three paragraphs, none longer than three sentences or 100 words.** The first paragraph introduces you, identifies the job and company, and then ends by briefly telling them why you are interested. The second paragraph tells them your credentials and why you are qualified. The last paragraph gives your contact details and asks for the job. I once found myself having to read a lot of cover letters and it drives me insane when they drone on and on for an entire page.

3) In an interview, think before answering every question and always prepare two questions ahead of time for your interviewer. You may Google for them but make sure they cannot be answered with a yes or no. If you cannot find a question with a question mark at the end, then make up a hypothetical situation based on what you assume about the job and simply set them going by asking "Do you agree?" The longer *they* talk, the better the interview goes. **At the end of the interview,**

always ask the same question, "So is there anything out there that you might think to be important that I did not think to ask?" If they say yes, you get something important. If they say no, you have covered everything that they have thought that you should have covered. Win-win.

4) In the office, listen to people and, if you have to, take notes while they talk. Do not just sit there and wait for them to finish talking. Instead, encourage them to talk and force yourself to listen. When someone does not feel like talking, wheedle them with compliments and get them comfortable. The more people the talk the better off you are. People will like you and you stay out of drama.

A bonus one for finance types and all others who work in "analyst" type jobs:

5 - Bonus!) Learn your Excel. Excel is the greatest application Microsoft ever created. It is elegant and efficient. Knowing your shortcuts and formulae can really make the day go by in a heartbeat. Finance people build huge Excel models that go on for pages and pages. It looks complex but the tools they use to build it are the same ones that everyone gets. A top Excel wizard can populate and format an entire worksheet without touching his mouse at all. Force yourself to keep your hands off that mouse! **Learn these two things in Excel right now: VLOOKUP and Pivot tables.** Open up Excel whenever you can and fiddle with those two. Google them, learn them and you can qualified for any job out there that requires Excel work.

So that is that. You would agree with me that it is not very inspirational stuff. They even seem pretty stupid at first glance but trust me, in the end you can go somewhere with these tips. Sometimes they fail. Sometimes they get me into trouble. Sometimes I feel like I should have gone the opposite way. Whatever. People win or lose by sticking to game plans so find something you can repeat over and over again and **stick with it**. Vacillating from one end of the pool to the other makes it real easy to find yourself gulping mouthfuls of chlorinated water.

So hang on there and push on.

A Short Moral Lesson That Did Not Take a Short Time to Learn

In the last section I told you four things that I always found to help me in my career. Now here is a brief moral lesson that I should have realized a long time ago but did not for many years. It is about life outside of work. I kind of imagine it this way: **The first section serves your physical needs - a job, house, etcetera - while the second minds the other stuff - family, health, and of course happiness.**

It comes in two numbers. Makes them easier to remember I suppose. Here they are:

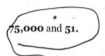

75,000 and 51.

That's about it. Have a good life everyone!

...

Just kidding.

You may already know what the first number means. It had been in the news. According to a study by the Woodrow Wilson School of Public Policy at Princeton,[65] $75,000 is the salary threshold where "the quality of [a person's] everyday emotional experiences" levels off. Up until then, salary matters. **Every dollar of salary you get while below the threshold, odds are it makes you a happier person.**

---

[65] The whole paper is in some big fancy psychology journal or what have you. However you can access a summary here at this URL:
http://wws.princeton.edu/news/Income_Happiness/Happiness_Money_Summary.pdf

Once you hit and go beyond the threshold though, your well being - happiness, sadness, enjoyment - levels off and the only thing more money brings you then is only a life that you think is better than someone else's. **A salary higher than $75,000 is only good for comparing yourself to other people.** And that, believe me, is climbing a ladder with no end.

So that is the first number. You have probably seen it blurbed somewhere. Kudos if you recognized it right off the bat. Now what does that second number mean?

51 is the average length in minutes of the American daily commute (a two way trip).[66] Now how and why does that matter? Simple. The longer your commute is, the unhappier you are going to be. Spending more time in the car driving down to work means you spend less time with other people. It results in more social isolation and in an unhealthier body. Some speculate that people choose jobs very far away because the money is good and they dismiss the idea of a long commute. It simply is not something people consider when they are job hunting.

So here I have come to a seemingly contradictory point: **Your career is not everything**. Money is not the only thing. There is a life out there for you to live and interests and passions that you should go out and pursue. Family, hobbies, a good book to read. Why not spend some of your time doing that instead of taking your work home every night on Friday? Things will work themselves out. You might worry about it, think

---

[66] I recommend this great article on commuting by the New Yorker:
http://www.newyorker.com/reporting/2007/04/16/070416fa_fact_paumgarten?currentPage=all

about it, and fuss a lot about it but **in the end it works itself out**. So keep that in mind. I never seem to be able to do so myself.

The end has arrived so I will be quick. Thank you, dear reader and best wishes for anything and everything you do.

Godspeed.

Acknowledgements

If you are reading this, you either know me personally or you found my personality so interesting that you are willing even to read this bland list of names to learn a little bit more about the mysterious author of this text. Odds are that you belong to the former than the latter.

As promised, what is going to follow is a bland list of names of which each individual entry means little or nothing to anyone except that of whom it is addressed towards. Turn back to less boring waters, you hath been warned.

First I would like to thank every person I have worked with and give them my heartfelt thanks for giving me the opportunity to learn from them. They are private people so I shall spare them the shame of having their names listed here. I will take my thanks to them in person. If you worked with me but have not heard of my thanks well then you were a terrible person and I do not want to talk to you.

...

Just kidding. It just means I have not gotten to you guys yet. Wait patiently and if you want to jump ahead in line like a collateralized bond ahead of a piece of mezzanine debt then you know how to reach me.

Second, I would like to thank everyone who took the time to read even a chapter or a page of this manuscript. Angela, Amick, April, Matt, and Rene.

Then there is my family. That's all that was needed to be said.

This book is dedicated to Jenny, even though she has never read it.

Footnotes Follow Here. That is all.

Made in the USA
Middletown, DE
06 July 2020